Communicating as a Professional Engineer

A Guide to Written and Oral Communication in the Business Environment

Edward E. Waldron
University of South Florida

KENDALL/HUNT PUBLISHING COMPANY
4050 Westmark Drive   Dubuque, Iowa 52002

Bridge image courtesy of Corel
Writing image © 2002 PhotoDisc, Inc.

Copyright © 2002 by Edward E. Waldron

ISBN 0-7872-9368-7

Kendall/Hunt Publishing Company has the exclusive rights to reproduce this work,
to prepare derivative works from this work, to publicly distribute this work,
to publicly perform this work and to publicly display this work.

All rights reserved. No part of this publication may be reproduced,
stored in a retrieval system, or transmitted, in any form or by any
means, electronic, mechanical, photocopying, recording, or otherwise,
without the prior written permission of Kendall/Hunt Publishing Company.

Printed in the United States of America
10 9 8 7 6 5 4 3 2 1

Contents

CHAPTER 1
　　Why Communications for Engineers? 1

CHAPTER 2
　　Ethics and Engineering 5

CHAPTER 3
　　Team Building: Creating a Business Context 13

CHAPTER 4
　　Memos and Reports 23

CHAPTER 5
　　Giving a Professional Oral Presentation 35

CHAPTER 6
　　Grammar and Usage 49

APPENDIX 1—ENGINEERING CODES OF ETHICS 63
　　Institute of Electrical and Electronics Engineers (IEEE)
　　　　Code of Ethics 63

　　American Society of Mechanical Engineers (ASME)
　　　　Code of Ethics of Engineers 64

　　National Society of Professional Engineers (NSPE)
　　　　Code of Ethics for Engineers 64

　　American Institute of Chemical Engineers
　　　　Code of Ethics 68

Association of Computing Machinery (ACM)
Code of Ethics   69

APPENDIX 2—ETHICAL SCENARIOS   75

1 | Why Communications for Engineers?

Engineers build bridges. Engineers create medical technologies. Engineers design and implement computer programs. Engineers fashion rocket engines to take us to the stars. So, why do engineers need to know how to write and speak effectively? Why can't they just do their scientific jobs and leave the communications to other people?

The simple fact is this: Engineers *do* have to be able to communicate effectively if they are to function in what is, after all, primarily a non-engineering world. They have to be able to explain their ideas and plans to several audiences, including city commissioners, clients, non-engineer colleagues, and even engineers from other disciplines. In the modern business world, no one can hide in a *Dilbert* cubicle and hope to be left alone.

One of the reasons Communications for Engineers was developed at the University of South Florida (USF) was that the USF College of Engineering requested such a course from the English department as an alternative to a regular technical writing course. Why? Because graduates working as engineers in the field said they could have used more preparation for writing and speaking in the business world in which they had to function.

This textbook is designed to serve as a guide for engineering students—and students in other technical disciplines—as they prepare to become contributing members of a business after graduation. The goal is not to make engineers great communicators, but to make them better, more aware writers and speakers. And that takes effort and hard work, especially for people who are inherently more comfortable with formulas than sentence patterns, who work more easily with numbers than with words.

FORMS OF COMMUNICATION

In the contemporary world of business, communications take place on many levels and make use of various approaches. In the course of a normal business day, an engineer might be called upon to draft:

- a memo to her boss regarding a project idea;
- an e-mail to a client setting up a meeting;
- a preliminary report on an ongoing construction site; and/or
- an oral presentation for another department on the model program being developed.

E-mail messages have become the communications glue that bonds businesses together. We draft them and send them, often without ever editing them. That may be acceptable for *some* internal messages, but can be dangerous for other purposes. Most e-mail programs now contain spell checkers to help catch glaring errors/typos, but as we will discuss later, spell checkers are not infallible. If you type "fell" instead of "feel," the spell checker is perfectly happy. The person receiving your communication might not be impressed, however. Sloppy communications efforts can imply a sloppy mind—definitely not the impression an engineer wants to create.

Businesses often live and die by the memos generated internally. They generally take more time—and reflect more thought—than e-mail messages. They can contain valuable information: statistics or preliminary evaluations from an ongoing project; important points to include in a bid for a contract; or background details on the people the boss will be meeting. Memos are more formal in style than e-mail messages, generally, but less involved than a formal report would be. The chapter on memos and reports provides some useful tips on creating a memo.

Many business reports can be conveyed in a memo format, especially reports that are no longer than two or three pages. More formal, developed reports, however, take on a form of their own. They require much more time to prepare and edit, and they have certain format requirements. In many instances, formal business reports are bound and treated as a booklet. Formal reports will have a title page and, even if they are brief, a table of contents and an executive summary.

Finally, engineers are, to their chagrin, often charged with making presentations to a variety of audiences, within the company and outside it. PowerPoint and other software programs have made the presenter's task easier in some ways. It is imperative to have some visuals in an oral presentation. Sometimes charts and graphs reproduced on posterboard will work nicely. In other situations, though, a dynamic slide show can make a presentation much more effective. Such productions add color and often movement to a mostly static speech. The trick is to find the right (and appropriate) balance between flair and effective communication. Too much color and movement in a slide show can be just as distracting and ineffective as a hard to read diagram on a too-small piece of posterboard. Some companies have begun to complain that their employees take too much time tinkering with their slide shows, simply because the programs make revisions so easy. Finding a proper balance of effort and need is also important.

Effective Writing vs. "Good" Writing

One problem for many people who are unsure of their writing ability is a tendency to "overwrite." It's the same impulse that leads people to say, "This responsibility belongs to him and I," instead of the grammatically correct, "This responsibility belongs to him and me." Why do people misuse the pronoun form like that? I suspect it is mainly because "I" *sounds* more proper and learned than "me." Yet that same person would never say, "This responsibility belongs to I."

Overwriting refers to using stilted word choice and often tortured sentence structure to try to affect a scholarly tone. Such an approach is bad enough in academic writing. In business writing, it is disastrous. A business person, especially a busy CEO, does not want to spend her time trying to decipher what a writer meant to say. The meaning should be clear and easy to detect. Burying thoughts in obtuse prose does nothing to further the cause of communication. The maxim KISS (keep it simple, stupid) applies as well to writing as to other areas of life.

10 Maxims to Maximize Your Writing Skills

Guiding Principles

1. Write unto others as you would have them write unto you.
2. When in doubt, think.

Getting Started

3. A beginning isn't set in stone—unless your thinking gets stonewalled.
4. Writing is not courtship—so get to the point quickly.

Be Concise

5. "Brevity is the soul of wit"—and an indicator of a clearly designed purpose.
6. In business writing, limitation is the sincerest form of flattery.

Be Precise

7. Just because something sounds "educated" doesn't mean it is correct.
8. Spill checkers have there limitations.

Maintain Perspective

9. *War and Peace* began as a blank sheet of paper.

Remember

10. Writing is a skill—and skills take practice.

First Impressions

Why is good writing so important to a professional? For one thing, it does no good to understand a concept or idea if you cannot communicate it to someone else who needs to understand it. For another, good writing can help prevent misunderstandings and confusion.

Perhaps even more important, however, is that your writing is often the first exposure another person has to you, whether it's an application for a job or a project proposal. Remember the old adage: You never get a second chance to make a first impression.

If your writing is logically sloppy and ill-thought out, or if your writing is filled with grammatical and typographical errors, it will reflect poorly on you as a possible employee. People who are themselves poor writers are often the harshest critics of the writing of others. So don't assume the human resources director of the company to which you are applying won't notice—or care—if you make a few mistakes. Would you want to hire an engineering firm to complete your pet project if the proposal they submit is full of misspelled words and sentences that make no sense?

Good writing *is* an important reflection of you as a professional person. It *does* make a difference.

TEAMWORK

A note on communications in a modern business setting: Communication is seldom a totally individual effort. Supervisors read and make editorial suggestions for much of what the people working under them create. Colleagues offer their opinions. The cleaning person might even leave a note on occasion. ("Just happened to notice you used the wrong pronoun in line 12. Shouldn't it be singular to agree with the subject? And please stop pouring your cold coffee in the wastebasket.")

Even more likely, however, is the possibility that projects will be assigned to teams of people in the company. You will need to function as a contributing member of those teams. Sometimes the tasks assigned will be job specific (e.g., as the engineer on the project, you design the mechanical system needed). Sometimes your task will be less clearly defined at the beginning, and you will create your own niche.

Depending on the size of your company and the nature of the project, you may work with several other engineers in your department. Or you may find yourself, as several professionals did at Hewlett Packard, assigned to a cross-discipline group (engineers, marketing people, production workers, shipping managers) to solve a specific problem for the company. The main point is, you will need to function within the group, contributing not only ideas from your own area of expertise, but also concepts for communicating those ideas outside the group.

For that reason, one of the very first chapters in this text involves setting up groups of students to work together to create a company, complete with logo, and completing a team project. There is often an initial reluctance to participate in group work. Some students may have had bad experiences with such efforts in the past. But semester after semester I have had students tell me how valuable they thought that team process was for them. And older students who have worked in business settings invariably agree that this is, in fact, how much of today's business projects get done in corporate America.

A FINAL THOUGHT

As is true in any other area of life, you will get out of this course what you put into it. If you approach the assignments and exercises in this text with a sense of adventure, rather than dread, you can have a meaningful and enjoyable course experience. But you must be prepared to work to make your writing better. That involves planning before you write, writing in as clear and direct a manner as possible, and, perhaps most importantly, proofreading and editing your work. The goal is not necessarily to "get it right" in the first draft—few people do. The goal is to "get it right" in the final draft, whether that is a second, third or (gasp) fourth draft.

As they say in prison movies, "If you work hard and follow directions, your time will go a lot better."

2

Ethics and Engineering

Engineering is a profession. It meets the criteria agreed upon by many observers who have tried to define what constitutes a profession. According to one such analyst, Michael D. Bayles, a profession has three central features:

- extensive training is required;
- that training has a "substantial intellectual component"; and
- the ability created by that training offers society an "important service."[1]

Engineering clearly meets those features. Bayles goes on to list other criteria: Professions require credentialing, generally offer organizations for members to join and give their practitioners some level of autonomy in their work. Again, engineering meets those criteria.

As professionals, engineers have duties they must fulfill, and those duties are best defined in the codes of ethics created by the various engineering societies. (Several of those codes are reproduced in Appendix 1.) Knowing what is expected of a person as a professional is one thing; however, deciding how to act ethically can be quite another matter. "Do what's right" is not always as simple as it sounds. Sometimes there are competing players in a scenario (colleagues, bosses, clients, the public) with competing claims for "right" actions that may or may not fit together.

This is a text on communications, not an ethics book. However, many of the most essential elements of effective communication have ethical components: honesty, fairness, and respect for the work of others, for example. Sometimes, bad writing results from sloppy thinking or unethical behavior. Neither reflects well on a professional person.

WHAT IS ETHICS?

Ethics can be defined in many ways and from many viewpoints. *Webster's New World Dictionary* offers a standard definition of "ethics": "the study of standards of conduct and moral judgment; moral philosophy."[2] The third definition offered, however, is more to our purpose: "the system or code of morals of a particular person, religion, group, [or] profession."

Michael Bayles refers to professional ethics as "a system of norms."[3] The focus in this approach to ethics is pragmatic. As Bayles notes, "Our concern is with what the behavior of professionals *should be* [my emphasis] rather than with what it is. ..." Codes of professional ethics, by and large, are guidelines, not "rules," as such. They tell the professional person how his or her profession believes its members *ought* to behave. As we will see, engineering as a profession has several codes of ethics to guide its members; some are general, some are for specific areas of engineering (e.g., civil or mechanical). All deal with certain core principles, such as honesty, fairness and confidentiality.

Ethical Principles for Engineers—The Base Values

We learn values from many sources over the course of our lives. Our family is the biggest shaper of values for most of us. Parents try to teach us right from wrong. We are taught the rules of conduct sent down from the parental mountain: Play nice with your brothers and sisters. Share your toys. Don't lie. Don't steal. Follow the Golden Rule. Other rules might also be set down, depending on the parents. And grandparents often talk about how things were in their day, when a simple handshake was more binding than a legal contract.

That is the ideal family world, perhaps more common on television shows from the 1950s and 1960s than the reality of the busy and diverse families of today. At any rate, the values instilled remain fairly universal. But the reality is, we learn quickly in our young lives, more often than not, that there are exceptions to these rules of moral behavior. Absolutes dissolve, quickly or slowly, in the broth of human experience.

Consider lying, for example—or rather its positive flip side, telling the truth. Our parents teach us to always tell the truth. If you were to ask 100 people whether telling the truth is an important virtue, 98 would probably say yes. By the same token, if you asked the same 100 people if they have never lied, maybe two would say they hadn't—and they'd probably be lying at the time. How can this be? Simple. From a very early age we learn that telling the truth can get us into BIG trouble.

If a vase is broken in the house and only two children are at home the time it happens, chances are one of them, perhaps both of them, did something to cause the vase to be broken. It doesn't matter whether the vase was broken accidently or after being used as a makeshift football. What matters is who gets blamed. And what follows disclosure is certain punishment. When confronted, child one denies any knowledge of a broken vase, while child two merely looks guilty and asks for mercy. Guess what happens. Child two gets grounded for a week and child one goes scot-free. If child one was, indeed, involved in the breakage, what lesson has he learned? Lying gets you off the hook. Child two learns a parallel lesson: Telling the truth can bring you misery.

Such lessons continue through childhood and into adult life. Telling the truth can get you sent to the principal's office or beaten up, or both. As an adult, it can cost you friends and more. For example, your best friend walks in wearing the most hideous hat you've ever seen and asks, beaming, what you think of it. The knee-jerk response is to lie and say it looks great. We refer to these moments as "white lies," a phrase that might be seen as racist and smacks of "good" magic (the antidote to "black" magic).

The point is, even for one of the most basic values—truth-telling—we learn there are exceptions in the course of our lives. We discover ways to bend the truth, to color it to answer a specific immediate need (I don't want to hurt Ann's feelings). Even more, we learn there are times when telling the truth may produce horrible personal consequences (Go to your room), when simply lying can save the day. The earth doesn't stop rotating. The birds still sing. Life goes on. We may feel a little guilty, for a while at least, but that, too, will pass. Of course, as recent political history has taught us, the truth *does* have a way of coming out, eventually. Denial may work, but usually only for a limited time. Spin can only carry a person so far.

The danger comes when some of our personal experiences with a moral value such as truth-telling influence our professional decision making. Lying to avoid a spanking or grounding as a child can carry over to lying about qualifications in order to get a desired job. (Is anyone *really* hurt?) Not telling a friend about a hideous clothing purchase can segue into hiding a minor design flaw from a client. (The project will still work.) While there may not be many absolutes in human behavior, we do need core values in our lives to function as a civilized culture.

Core Values

The Professional Engineering Practice Liaison Program (PEPL) at the University of Washington's College of Engineering published on its Web site the following recommended core ethical values, based on research completed in 1996.[4] The core values are presented as a way of bringing applied ethics into a professional practice to help engineers develop solutions to ethical dilemmas encountered in professional practice.

Those core values are:

1. Integrity, including:
    a. exercising good judgment in professional practice
    b. adherence to ethical principles

2. Honesty, including:
    a. truthfulness
    b. fairness
    c. sincerity

3. Fidelity, including:
    a. faithfulness to clients
    b. allegiance to the public trust
    c. loyalty to employer, firm or agency
    d. loyalty to the profession
    e. for the theist, faithfulness to God

4. Charity, including:
    a. kindness
    b. caring
    c. good will
    d. tolerance
    e. compassion/mercy
    f. adherence to the Golden Rule

5. Responsibility, including:
    a. reliability/dependability
    b. accountability
    c. trustworthiness

6. Self-Discipline, including:
    a. acting with reasonable restraint
    b. not indulging in excessive behavior.

Many of these core values resonate with all of us because they echo the values we've grown up with: Be kind, show tolerance and compassion, follow the Golden Rule. Those values cut across religious and cultural lines.

Some of these values, however, have a specific application to a person in a professional position. Fidelity, for example, speaks to how a professional relates to those he or she works with and for: clients, the public, employers, the profession itself. In ethics, we often speak of rights and duties. If one person or group has rights (e.g., to have confidences respected), the professionals who serve that person or group have a corresponding duty, in this case to respect the client's confidentiality and guard confidential information. Showing "faithfulness to clients" entails more than respecting the client's confidences, however. The concept also embraces the idea that a professional will see a job through or, if unable to complete the job for some reason, see that another qualified person can take over and complete it. Each of these core values has a wealth of possible interpretations.

> ### EXERCISE ONE
>
> 1. Select one of the core values listed above and explain how it might be reflected in the work of an engineer.
> 2. Choose one of the case studies in Appendix 2 and discuss how one or more of the core values might be involved in a solution to the question(s) raised.

CODES OF ETHICS FOR ENGINEERS

There are several professional societies to which engineers might belong. Some, such as the National Society of Professional Engineers (NSPE), are general in scope; others, such as the American Society of Civil Engineers (ASCE), are geared toward members of specific engineering disciplines. Examples of these and other professional societies' codes of ethics can be found in Appendix 1.

A close examination of these codes reveals many similarities—and some interesting differences. Most of those differences have to do with specific issues that arise from a particular discipline (e.g., computer engineering). Certain areas of concern resonate in these codes, especially concerns about public safety and well-being and the engineer's duties (1) to protect the public against faulty design or workmanship and (2) to maintain and foster a responsible attitude toward the environment.

The language used in the codes is often duplicated. The NSPE Code of Ethics, for example, lists as its first fundamental canon that engineers should "hold paramount the safety, health, and welfare of the public." The American Society of Mechanical Engineers (ASME) Code of Ethics repeats the core idea verbatim: "Engineers shall hold paramount the safety, health, and welfare of the public in the performance of their duties." The Institute of Electrical and Electronics Engineers (IEEE) Code of Ethics uses a slightly different wording. IEEE members agree "to accept responsibility in making engineering decisions consistent with the safety, health, and welfare of the public, and to disclose promptly factors that might endanger the public or the environment."

This pattern of repeated language underscores the importance of certain key principles to all engineering disciplines. Other principles repeated throughout the codes include honesty and competence, for example. Canon 3 of the NSPE Code of Ethics and Canon 7 in the ASME code state that engineers should "issue public statements only in an objective and truthful manner." The NSPE code adds, in Canon 7, that engineers should "avoid deceptive acts." The IEEE code tells members "to be honest and realistic" when making claims or using data. The code of ethics for the Association of Computer Machinery (ACM) has members agree to "be honest and trustworthy." Several of the codes (NSPE, IEEE, ASCE and ASME) remind engineers that they are to operate only "in areas of their competence." That last might seem self-evident, but consider the pressure an engineer working for a small firm might come under to take on a job outside her expertise, "to help out." These principles exist for good reasons.

Finding a Solution to an Ethical Dilemma

If there is only one clear action to take in order to be ethical, then we know pretty clearly what we should do in a particular situation. We may not always take that action, but at least we know we are acting unethically if we go counter to it. But, more often than not, there is no clear, single action marked with a huge "Ethical" sign. We may see several options available and not be sure which is the most ethical to choose. That's called an ethical dilemma: when there are two (or more) actions to consider, both (or all) of which can be argued as ethical responses. How can that be?

For one thing, situations we encounter in professional life usually involve more than one person or group—the public, our employers, our colleagues. Each of those persons or groups may have a claim on our behavior that says we should act in their favor. The code of ethics we follow may tell us, for example, to "always act in the best interests of the client." That same code, however, may also tell us to "act in ways to protect the environment." What if what our client requires from us (e.g., to build a structure in a specific location) conflicts with the protection of the environment (i.e., the structure needs to be built in an environmentally fragile area)? What action can we take that will fulfill both our ethical duty to the client and our ethical duty to the environment? How do we decide what to do?

Obviously, if there are laws that limit certain actions (such as prohibiting the erection of a structure on a protected piece of land), we are bound as good citizens to obey those laws. Laws are not always clear, though, and there may be some leeway in what action we take. The area may be fragile, but not officially "protected," for example.

Several guides such as the one below have been developed to help individuals approach making an ethical decision in a rational, reasoned way. All of them include a series of steps to follow. The process allows a person to weigh factors and attempt to develop clarity about what the issue at stake really is. Sometimes, what we *think* is the problem is not. The essential point to remember is that other people can be affected by the ethical decisions *you* make. Let's consider the process, step by step.

1. Establish the facts of the situation.

Determining what "really" happened or what "really" is at stake in a situation is not always easy. It is important to try to understand as many of the facts as you can gather, so that you will be making an informed decision. Sometimes we discover in a reasoned assessment of the facts that what we thought was an ethical dilemma really is not. It becomes clear that there is only one ethical course of action.

Example: An engineer negotiating a contract might be considering whether to pay a bribe to an official in a foreign country in order to get a favorable review because she has been led to believe that is the way things are done there. Her company needs the job to stay viable, so there is a possible tension between "rejecting bribery" and being loyal to the company. Some research shows, however, that what has been represented as a "standard business practice" in this culture is actually frowned upon in that country, just as it would be in the United States. It becomes clear from the "facts" that the ethical choice is not to offer a bribe.

2. Identify the stakeholders.

A "stakeholder" is anyone who might be affected by the decision made in an ethical dilemma. The individual making the decision is obviously a stakeholder. So is the company he works for and the client involved. Sometimes, it is important to pull back even further, however, to include stockholders in the company who might lose or gain financially as a result of the decision made. The general public might be a stakeholder in a decision that involves an environmental issue. The key is to try to be as complete as possible in identifying any person or group that might benefit—or suffer—from the decision made.

Example: A plant is dumping waste materials into a community water source. Some of those materials might be toxic. The person who discovers the problem needs to consider several steps. It might seem obvious

Resolving Ethical Dilemmas
An Eight-Step Approach

1. **Establish the facts of the situation.**

   Be as specific as possible. Avoid bias as much as possible.

2. **Identify the stakeholders.**

   Who has an interest in the outcome of the situation? Be as inclusive as possible.

3. **Understand the stakeholders' motivation.**

   What does each person have to gain (or lose) from the decision being made?

4. **Construct alternative solutions to the dilemma.**

   Using a relevant code of ethics and the best information available, what ethical solutions can be constructed and supported?

5. **Weigh the alternative solutions being proposed.**

   Weed out any solutions that cannot be supported ethically. Focus on the most ethically sound alternatives and determine which has the greatest ethical value.

6. **Select the best solution.**

   It may be necessary to revisit steps 1–5 several times before reaching a conclusion.

7. **Act on the solution chosen.**
8. **Assess/evaluate the outcome.**

that the person should immediately notify the Environmental Protection Agency or a state agency to determine whether the material is indeed toxic. But before that step is taken, he should consider the stakeholders involved in the decision. As an engineer, he has an ethical duty to protect the environment. And the public welfare also must be considered. The people who own or work for the company, however, also have a stake in his decision, as do any stockholders. Here is a situation in which simply gathering the facts might impact different stakeholders. An internal investigation might resolve the issue without affecting stakeholders. A public investigation could have negative consequences, however, even if there is no harm being done.

3. Understand the stakeholders' motivation.

What does each person have to gain (or lose) from the decision being made? Sometimes that answer is clear and obvious. Your client might gain a new plant more cheaply if you take shortcuts on some safety issues. Your company will benefit from having this client's business. You might have a shot at a promotion if this deal comes through. What might not be so clear, however, are the "motivations" of other stakeholders. The employees who will work at that plant want a safe working environment. Consumers who buy products made at that plant want products that work as they are supposed to. Those are "motivations," too.

It isn't always easy to examine a situation and develop a clear picture. And motivations are not always evil or driven by greed. The client might want a cheaper plant built so she can produce goods at a more reasonable price and benefit her stockholders. Employees at the plant might willingly work in a plant that is a little shy of strict requirements if it means higher pay and better job security. Resolving an ethical dilemma often requires some very careful weighing of factors.

4. Construct alternative solutions to the dilemma.

Using a relevant code of ethics and the best information available, what ethical solutions can be constructed and supported? There is often more than one solution available to resolve an ethical dilemma. One solution may favor one stakeholder over another, based on a legitimate ethical claim. A second solution may favor a different stakeholder, based again on a supportable ethical standard. The challenge at this stage is to remain open-minded enough to see several alternative solutions.

5. Weigh the alternative solutions being proposed.

Weed out any solutions that cannot be supported ethically. Focus on the most ethically sound alternatives and determine which has the greatest ethical value. If we are lucky, one solution soon begins to assume obvious weight over the others. Stakeholder one's claim to the right to a safe working environment, for example, assumes more weight, supported by clear ethical reasoning, than stakeholder two's claim to expect a profit from investing in a company.

6. Select the best solution.

It may be necessary to revisit steps 1–5 several times before reaching a conclusion. The key is to be comfortable that the solution chosen offers a valid ethical approach to resolving the dilemma—and can be supported by logical reasoning.

7. Act on the solution chosen.

Once you have made the decision, then you must act on it. This may require explaining your decision to several different stakeholders. Or it may be a completely internalized decision upon which you act. If you have involved others in the decision-making process, then you should also let them know what you've decided—and why.

8. Assess/evaluate the outcome.

It is always a good rule to evaluate decisions you have made—whether they are ethically based or simply standard business decisions. Did the decision work out as you anticipated? Was the result what you had hoped it would be? Were there complications you hadn't anticipated that should be factored into any future decisions? We all make mistakes. The important thing is to learn from them so we can avoid repeating them. Don't expect yourself to be perfect—but never stop trying to be a logical decision maker.

I think you will find this process a useful tool for helping you resolve ethical dilemmas. It provides a *logical* approach, a reasoned approach, that helps avoid the hand-wringing with which we often confront ethical problems.

On the other hand, resolving an ethical crisis is *not* like using a formula to determine the maximum allowable weight for a bridge support. You need to approach the two differently. The point is to take *both* problems seriously as a professional engineer.

WRITING ASSIGNMENT #1

Choose one of the following topics:

1. Select one of the codes of ethics in Appendix 1 and write a brief analysis of it. Don't just repeat the principles or canons listed. Look at what the code stresses in the behavior of an engineer: Are there certain words/principles that have obvious weight? Are they connected? Where does the ethical engineer owe certain duties (e.g., the public, employer)? Construct a topic sentence that clarifies the point of your analysis and write a paragraph (one page or less) developing that topic sentence.
2. Select two of the codes of ethics in Appendix 1 and compare them in a brief (one page) analysis. How are they similar? Where do they differ? Does one code stress a particular principle more than the other?
3. Select one of the case studies in Appendix 2 and discuss how you would resolve the situation outlined. A one-page analysis should be sufficient. Be sure to consider the steps discussed above.

Notes

[1] Michael D. Bayles, *Professional Ethics*, second edition (Belmont, CA: Wadsworth Publishing Company, 1989), p. 8.
[2] Second College Edition (New York: Simon and Schuster, 1980), p. 481.
[3] Bayles, p. 17.
[4] "Recommended Core Ethical Values," *Applied Ethics Case of the Month Club*. Professional Engineering Practice Liaison Program, College of Engineering, University of Washington. 6 February 2001. http://www.engr.washington.edu/~uw-epp/Pepl/Ethics/ethics3.html.

3

Team Building: Creating a Business Context

In 1996, *Fortune* magazine profiled an extraordinary experiment at Hewlett Packard.[1] The high-tech giant had a problem: The company was taking an average of 26 days between receipt of a product order and delivery. Order information had to pass through 70 computer systems (some more than 10 years old). Basically, the company faced the same problem other U.S. companies were facing. The economy was changing rapidly, and old ways of doing business simply weren't effective enough anymore.

To tackle this problem, HP assigned two managers to put together an interdisciplinary team of 35 people from within HP, Andersen Consulting and Menlo Logistics, HP's transportation and distribution partner. The goal was to reengineer the company's existing system into a unified database that could track orders through delivery. The team was given nine months to create a solution. They reached their goal in eight months. Average product delivery time dropped from 26 days to eight days.

How did they do it? The managers wiped out titles and old expectations within the team and let the team members figure out what to do. At first such freedom was disturbing. But team members learned to break the larger problem into smaller, more manageable ones. They practiced their proposed solutions to see what worked and what didn't. As one team leader, Julie Anderson, said, "You've got to start without knowing where the journey is going to take you."[2] That is not always easy to do, of course. We fear the unknown. On the other hand, the "unknown" is where new discoveries dwell.

Other companies have also found that using teams can provide many benefits, from bringing experts from different departments together to solve a common problem, as HP did, to improving morale by creating a sense of ownership among employees. The simple fact is, in the modern business setting, employees often find themselves drawn into a team situation. Learning to work well with others is as important in your professional life as it was in kindergarten.

> "A camel looks like a horse that was planned by a committee."
> *Vogue* magazine, July 1958

In spite of what many people think, committees are not necessarily an ineffective forum for conducting business. Put together thoughtfully and managed with skill, they can be quite productive, as we see in the HP example. How to assemble the committee—or team: That's the challenge.

TEAM BUILDING—PLAYGROUND STYLE

Remember playing sports when you were a kid? Two people, usually the best athletes on the playground, would choose sides, picking one kid at a time. The good players always went first, and the rest of us ordinary mortals were taken (often reluctantly) toward the end. The idea, of course, was to put together the best team one could. The fastest, best catching, hitting or throwing kids were picked early; the weaker ones were taken last to round out the team. In baseball, the worst player was usually sent to the purgatory of right field, where few if any balls were ever hit. The best players pitched or played shortstop or center field. The best hitters led off or batted third or fourth; the worst hitter batted ninth.

These makeshift groups were "teams" only in the most literal sense of the word—i.e., the opposing groups in baseball are called "teams." They weren't really teams in the *best* sense of the word: a group of people working together in concert to solve a common problem. The selection process was very arbitrary. If your best friend was a team captain, at least you'd get picked. If you were a weak player, your only chance was that the numbers needed meant you *had* to be picked. (Better a bad player than no player in right field.) Personalities often dominated the selection process. If you were liked, even if you weren't a super player, you'd get picked, too.

The "teams" thus temporarily assembled had no loyalties beyond the day—beyond the game itself. After the game, the "team" disbanded. If there was a new game the next day, the "team" might have a completely different makeup, depending on who was there and the order of selection.

That fluidity in the team process has its advantages. If the team doesn't work well together today, a new team can be put together tomorrow. If you don't get the best pitcher on your team for this game, you might get him or her for the next one. And if you really don't like most of the kids on your team today, there's always a chance you'll have some friends on the team tomorrow.

But there are also disadvantages to constantly shifting team membership. You don't get a chance to develop ways of working better together, for instance. If mistakes are made during the current game, you might not get the opportunity to rectify them with a new group the next day. Bonding can't take place under those circumstances, at least not beyond the bonds that already exist between friends. Worst of all, this method of "team-building" often means that weaker players never really get a chance to improve, to grow beyond their existing abilities. The assumptions that dominate the selection process (e.g., Tim can't catch anything) take on a life and "truth" of their own.

Unfortunately, the playground approach to team-building extends beyond childhood games. If students are asked to form groups in a class, for example, the almost automatic response is for friends to group together. That may be more difficult in college, where students are often strangers to one another, but it still happens. The impulse is to form a group with others who are like you (e.g., people you know from other classes, sorority sisters, other athletes). Obviously, that approach brings with it a certain comfort level. But it sacrifices an opportunity that is at the center of the college experience: exploring differences and learning from them.

In business, managers may also find it easier to assemble teams by putting only their "best" staff members together. The rationale is startlingly similar to the playground method of selection: Only those we "know" to be the best players should be selected. And we find it hard to think beyond the box. If we have an engineering problem, we should have a team of engineers to work on it. If the problem is in production, we should have a team of production workers address the issue.

The HP example that began this chapter, however, suggests something different. It suggests that putting people from different disciplines together to solve a problem can lead to a new solution that no one discipline may have discovered on its own. That engineering problem may have a marketing solution. The production quandary might be solved through a change in product distribution. The point is, we often can not know in advance *where* the answer to a problem might be found. The broader our scope of inquiry—and the broader our pool of individuals working on the problem—the better our chances for finding the solution.

AN ALTERNATIVE PROCESS

Several projects in this text call for a team approach. I have found the most useful way to form teams is a *controlled* random selection. Let me explain.

Students fill out the form below and hand it in. I then begin a process of assembling mixed teams of students.

```
Name _____

Major area _____


Level of computer expertise/knowledge of
PowerPoint _____
_____
```

Figure 1: Student Information Form

After collecting the information sheets from the students, I make piles according to major area (mechanical engineering, electrical engineering, computer science). Then I start forming groups of five students each, trying to mix the areas of major emphasis as much as possible. (Sometimes it is difficult to avoid having two or more students from the same major in a group, of course.)

In the next step, I try to ensure that there is at least one female student in each group. The growth of women entering the engineering field has made this much easier. The diversity of the work force is being reflected in the professional schools and that diversity offers students a chance for a rich learning experience.

The final consideration in putting groups together is to make sure each group has at least one student who has computer experience, especially using PowerPoint or similar programs. Group presentations will be done using PowerPoint, and it is helpful if someone in the group has experience using the software. (In a class of engineering students, this rarely poses a problem.) Most presentation software, including PowerPoint, is easy to navigate, and learning to use it is an important skill for anyone going into the business world.

Putting groups together this way mirrors the HP team process and keeps students from teaming up with people they know. It gives them the chance to interact with students from different engineering majors and perhaps see other ways to approach solving problems. An added advantage is the mix of international students majoring in engineering. Getting to know students from other cultures can be a great benefit to engineers entering an increasingly international business world. It enriches the learning experience for everyone.

The first order of business, once the teams are put together, is for team members to introduce themselves. In addition to sharing names and majors, students need to provide their teammates ways to contact them outside of class—e-mail addresses, phone number(s) or both. That way if a student knows he or she will miss class during a team project session, teammates can be notified, and the student who misses class can be brought up to speed on the team's progress.

After the "getting to know you" process is completed, it's on to the fun part of the initial team project. To lend some credibility and purpose to the team concept, each team creates a company, complete with (1) name, (2) logo, (3) mission statement, (4) code of ethics and (5) flow chart.

CREATING A BUSINESS CONTEXT—WHAT'S IN A NAME?

The first order of business is to come up with company name. That is not as easy as it may sound. A few preliminary steps are essential. Before a team can settle on a name for its company, it needs to decide what *kind* of company it will be. It could be:

- a construction company;
- a consulting firm;
- a computer software company;
- an environmental safety company;
- an aerospace firm; or
- a manufacturing company.

The possibilities are almost endless. Ideally, of course, the company should have *some* engineering component involved. Once the team has decided what its company will do, then it can begin the process of selecting a name.

The following suggestions might help. The company name should:

- be imaginative and innovative;
- link easily to what the company does; and
- be original (i.e., not an existing company name).

The first two parts require some creativity. The third part requires some research, although a rather limited amount of research in this case.

Individually, students may not feel they are creative. One of the benefits of working in a team, however, is that we can often be inspired by the people we are working with. Ideas can build off one another. It is important to treat this as a brainstorming session: Listen to all proposals, however far-fetched or impractical, and try to make sure everyone gets involved.

Getting reluctant or inherently quiet students involved in exercises such as this can be a challenge for the other students. Type A students, especially, might find it difficult to allow some free-roaming discussions during this first project. Sometimes the temptation is to jump in and take control or to press the others to make decisions. But it is important to let the ideas flow. Often a very creative name pops out when least expected.

One test for the feasibility of a proposed name is how much it indicates (or at least suggests) what this company does, or the product or service it provides. Using a team member's name for the company is an easy out, and it rarely can suggest a company's area of expertise. A way to work around this limitation is to create a catch phrase to put under the name:

- "Computer software to meet *your* needs"
- "Building bridges for the future"
- "Solving environmental problems since 1978."

Even with a company name that makes clear a company's focus, a catch phrase can help draw a potential client's attention.

The pinnacle of successful naming is achieved in those rare instances when a particular company's product name becomes synonymous with the product itself. When you need to blow your nose, what do you ask for—a tissue or a Kleenex? For many people, a "Coke" can be any soft drink. And how often do we "Xerox" copies on duplicating machines made by another company? Sometimes this phenomenon can be attributed to the fact that a company's product was the first in its field. More often, however, it's likely due to an effective advertising campaign.

For our purposes, the concern with not infringing on existing copyrighted or trademarked names can be limited to simply not picking a known company name: no "Nike Construction," for example. A brief search on the Internet might also tell you whether a company with the same name you want to use actually exists.

> A word of caution: In the "real" world, a company would need to do extensive research—or, more likely, hire a firm specializing in such matters—to ensure there was not an existing company with the same name.

What's Your Sign? Creating a Company Logo

An appealing or intriguing logo can help establish a company's identity in the minds of potential clients. Like the company name, the logo should:

- be imaginative and innovative;
- link easily to what the company does; and
- be original (i.e., not an existing logo).

Creating a corporate logo is even more of a creative challenge at times than coming up with a company name. Sometimes, however, the choice of a logo flows naturally from the company name itself.

If your company's name—or its catch phrase—suggests an image (e.g., "Building bridges for the future"), then the logo might utilize that image. Let's say, for example, that your company is a consulting firm that is set up to help other companies solve problems. Maybe your company's catch phrase is "Putting the pieces together for you" or "Helping your company solve puzzling problems." The following piece of clip art suggests one possible logo—or part of a logo:

Many companies combine a catch phrase and logo as part of the company letterhead. Your class company may decide to do the same thing, and use letterhead stationery for the brief report memos developed from your

Figure 2: From Corel WordPerfect Suite 8 Clip Art

part of team projects. (Just make sure the image can be imported into the word processing program you are using.)

As with the company name, teams should be sure not to duplicate an existing logo: no Nike "swoosh" or interlocking McDonald's arches. Clip art can certainly provide usable images for a logo. Many Internet sites are devoted to clip art images that can be downloaded and used free. If a team member has an artistic bent, perhaps your company can develop original art to use as a logo. Just remember to keep the image as clean and simple as possible. It's no accident that the Nike logo is so readily recognizable.

This is *not* a design class. You aren't expected to create a professional logo for your company. Have some fun with this part of the assignment—but don't get too carried away.

THE MISSION STATEMENT

A company's mission statement can serve several purposes:

- It can be a declaration of the promises the company makes to its customers/clients: "We guarantee all our work to your satisfaction."
- It can enunciate goals to which the company aspires: "We will be the best telecommunications company in the United States."
- It can combine promises and goals.

Many of the items listed in a company's mission statement are directed toward customers/clients. Other items may be directed toward employees. Basically, a mission statement says: This is what our company stands for; this is how we would like to be perceived.

For our purposes, the mission statement developed for your company can be brief. Basically, it should reflect how your firm relates to clients, its employees and/or the public. The language should be simple and direct. Avoid rhetorical flourishes; make your statements in plain English.

CREATIVE BUILDING DESIGNS MISSION STATEMENT

Creative Building Designs makes the following pledge. We will:

1. Complete all work on time and within budget.
2. Treat our clients with respect and honesty.
3. Protect the environment as we complete our job.
4. Encourage our employees to continue their professional growth.

Sample Company Mission Statement

Many companies display their mission statement for public view. Some display them where employees can see them on a regular basis, e.g., in a break room or conference room. The important idea is to *have* a mission statement and to be sure employees know it exists. A well-crafted mission statement can be a source of encouragement and pride for employees. It can set the tone for the way in which a company conducts its business. The most important factor, of course, is how well a company puts into practice the pledge(s) made.

THE CODE OF ETHICS

As professionals, engineers are expected to follow the guidelines of the code of ethics governing their particular field of engineering—or engineering in general. Those codes establish what is acceptable—indeed, expected—behavior for engineers as they carry out their professional duties. As we saw in Chapter Two, the various codes of ethics for engineering societies have many similarities in what they establish as an accepted pattern of behavior for members.

Many companies also have a code of ethics. Depending on the type of company, the code of ethics may be specifically geared toward engineers, or it may be more general, to include all employees working for the firm. In any case, a code of ethics establishes a company's guidelines for employee behavior.

As was the case with the mission statement, the code of ethics developed for in-class team companies should be fairly brief. It can also make use of bullet points to highlight the company's expectations of employee behavior toward clients, competitors and each other. The engineering societies' codes of ethics students analyzed in Chapter Two's assignment can serve as models for the company code of ethics.

A company's code of ethics is often displayed side-by-side with its mission statement. The parallels between the two documents help emphasize a company's dedication to key principles of honesty and hard work. Clients

> ### CREATIVE BUILDING DESIGNS CODE OF ETHICS
>
> **The employees of Creative Building Designs pledge to:**
>
> 1. Treat all clients fairly and honestly.
> 2. Protect the confidences of every client.
> 3. Respect the work of our competitors.
> 4. Refuse any form of bribery.
> 5. Do our best to represent the company as good citizens/employees.

Sample Code of Ethics

and employees alike can find comfort and inspiration in such documents—if the firm is clearly dedicated to making them work effectively.

THE COMPANY FLOW CHART

As part of the exercise for student teams to form their own company, developing a flow chart for the company can add a final sense of completion. Students who have been employed or are currently employed outside school may be familiar with the concept of a flow chart.

A flow chart (or organizational chart) is, basically, a graphic representation of a company's hierarchy. It delineates the "pecking order" of the firm, i.e., who reports to whom. It helps clarify relationships among and between departments in a large company and establishes a chain of command. At the top sits the CEO or Chief Executive Officer or President or Chairman. The title of the person who heads a company can vary. Some firms use Chief Executive Officer; some simply use CEO. In one company, the person may be designated Chairman of the Board of Directors that runs the company; in another, he or she may be the Chairman, President *and* CEO.

Under that person come the various vice presidents who head company departments. Some firms have an executive vice president who stands between the CEO/President and the vice presidents. There might also be a Chief Financial Officer (CFO) and/or a Chief Information Officer (CIO). The permutations are as varied as the companies that make up corporate America. For purposes of this course, student teams only need to develop a two-tiered flow chart incorporating the CEO and vice presidents. To simplify the process, the instructor can serve as the CEO of all companies in the class. (After all, the instructor will be the recipient of all the reports generated during the semester.) Team members can assume titles of departmental vice presidents.

Exactly what departments the student company has will depend largely on the type of company it is. All companies will have a human resources (HR) department, for example, but only a manufacturing firm would need a shipping department. The company might have a research and development (R&D) department and a marketing department, whether it is manufacturing or service oriented.

Programs such as Microsoft's PowerPoint and Corel's Presentations can both be used to generate a flow chart.

A Final Word on Creating a Business Context

The process outlined in this chapter has two purposes. One is to involve students in putting the barest beginnings of a company together. We only covered the easy parts, but financing a new business and creating a customer base are well outside the scope of this course.

The second, and more important purpose, is to get students engaged in the group process. Learning to work together and break a project into manageable parts should help the teams established during this exercise complete the team projects to come. Some of the reports covered in the next chapter have both team and individual components.

Notes

[1] Stratford Sherman, "Secrets of HP's 'Muddled' Team," *Fortune* (March 18, 1996), p. 116.
[2] Sherman, p. 120.

4

Memos and Reports

The bulk of communications in the contemporary workplace takes place through memos, reports, and e-mails. The cartoons that show co-workers in adjoining cubicles communicating via e-mails—as opposed to standing up and chatting—are not far-fetched. This chapter will concentrate on memos and reports. As you will see, brief reports can often be conveyed in a memo format. The business memo has an important place in the overall scheme of intra- and inter-office communications, whether in printed form or conveyed as attachments to e-mail. Writing effective memos can be as challenging as writing the most involved research paper. The result may be much shorter, but the content has to be more carefully developed *because* of that brevity.

THE ART OF THE BUSINESS MEMO

The business memorandum still plays an important role in most companies. It is a short, written record that can be used to convey a wide range of information and ideas. Because it can be used in a printed or an electronic form, it has a versatility that a bound formal report does not. By its very nature, a memo should be brief and very tightly focused. It should be about one subject—and one only. The key to an effective memo lies in its organization and clarity of purpose.

Memos can discuss the progress being made on a project or propose an approach to a problem that the company faces. There are several standard formats for a business memo, but the subject matter they contain is fairly open. A general rule of thumb is that a memo should not be more than two or three pages long. Any subject requiring more than that space should probably be conveyed in a full report format.

A basic memo format looks like the following:

> # MEMO
>
> To: Your recipient(s)
> From: Your name
> Date: The date
> Subject: A precise statement of the memo's subject/purpose
>
> Text, including bullet lists, charts, graphs and other forms of information. Use standard margins and pay attention to the layout of the memo. Make it easy to read and pleasing to the eye. The *look* of a memo can make the recipient more receptive to its message.

Figure 1: Typical Memo Format

Word and other writing programs offer variations on this format. Some invert the Date and Subject lines; some leave a space between the Date and Subject lines. Some use Re (regarding), instead of Subject. For our purposes, the form above works fine. If you work for a company that uses a specific style for its memos, then you should, of course, follow that format.

The most important element of a memo is its Subject line (the other three lines pretty much take care of themselves). A memo's Subject line has to convey what the memo is about in a way that the recipient clearly understands. It should be informative, but brief. Remember: The person receiving your memo is most likely getting several other memos at the same time. You should make it easy for her to fit your memo into her reading priority. Effective communication does not involve a guessing game.

Consider these three subject lines:

1. Subject: Building Inspection
2. Subject: Fire Safety Inspection
3. Subject: Cooper Hall Fire Safety Inspection

Number 1 is too generalized to be useful. Number 2 is a little better, but still not building specific. Number 3, however, tells its recipient *what* building was inspected and *which* area of inspection is involved in this particular memo. It is still brief, but it is specific. That's what a good Subject line should be.

Because most of the reports written in this course will be relatively brief, they can be done in memo format. The formal report, which is your final assignment, will be too long to be in a memo; we will discuss its formatting separately. We will have three memo assignments: an inspection report, a trip report, and a recommendation report. One other assignment, written instructions, will not be in memo form. It should basically be a written version of the oral presentation outlined in Chapter 5.

For all assignments, use a 12-point font such as Arial or Times New Roman. Single space the text and double space between paragraphs and headings.

Inspection Report

The first memo assignment for the course parallels the first oral presentation (see Chapter 5). As is the case for the oral presentation, each student is responsible for reporting his/her part of the overall inspection performed by the team. The information should be essentially the same as that given in the oral presentation. What is different is the mode of transmitting the information.

Once your team has made the inspection and you have decided how to divide up the report, you can put your part of the inspection together in a memo. Remember, such a report can be positive in nature. If a building meets general access requirements, for example, it is certainly permissible to give it a positive report in that area.

If you do report negative conditions, however, be prepared to offer recommendations for improving the problems you find, both in the oral presentation and in the written report. The recommendations should be practical and achievable, given the money to carry them out. In other words, razing the building and starting from scratch will probably *not* be workable options. The recommendations section is an important part of your written assignment related to the building inspection.

The general look of the memo should be based on the sample given above. (Remember: The subject line should be specific without being longer than a single line.) Think of the layout of the memo in three stages:

- an introductory paragraph;
- a section of observations (positive and negative); and
- a recommendation section (where applicable).

That's a fairly standard development scheme for any expository writing: introduction, body and conclusion.

Introductory Paragraph

In the memo's first paragraph you should make clear two key points:

1. Why is the person receiving this memo?
2. What is it about?

A standard opening to a business memo usually clarifies why the person is receiving the memo. Often, the memo comes in response to some request for information or action:

On September 5, 2001, you asked our company to do a thorough inspection of Cooper Hall on the USF Tampa campus.

or

This memo is a response to your request of April 5, 2001, for a progress report on the Jacksonville construction project.

A beginning such as this serves as a gentle reminder that the person asked for this information. You aren't just presenting it out of the blue.

The rest of the initial paragraph in your inspection report memo should indicate two important points: (1) that the complete inspection is being reported in sections and (2) that *your* memo concerns one specific part of the whole. (This memo focuses on general safety issues; other issues will be addressed in memos from the rest of the inspection team.) This clarification lets the recipient know that your memo is only one piece of the total report and that he/she should be alert for the other reports.

(**Note:** A report such as this done in the real business world would be presented as a whole. What the person would receive is a complete report that integrates all the team members' findings in one seamless report. We are using the separate memos primarily for grading purposes.)

Observations

This is the section in which you report the observations you made during the inspection. Those observations can be positive or negative. It's possible that a building will be in good shape in one category or another, and that can be acknowledged as well as problems. The idea of such a report is to present an overall picture of the building's condition (from what is a superficial examination, of course).

If you do find both positive and negative observations to report, it is a good idea to create subsections for each, so your reader knows which is which immediately. Otherwise, if you combine both into a single list, the details could get blurred and confusing. With both positive and negative conditions to report, it's best to give the positive first. That way, there is a closer connection between the *negative* conditions reported in this section and the *recommendations* for improvements to come. Always consider the logic of arranging your details.

The key to this section is to provide enough details to make the observations clear to your reader. This isn't creative writing, but you will need to use some adjectives and other descriptors. Just don't get carried away. Remember: This is an objective business report. A little goes a long way.

You also need to set up each list you use in this section. By that, I mean you should introduce what the list contains. For example:

> *During our inspection of the business building, we noticed the following positive conditions regarding fire safety:*

Then you provide a bullet list of those observations. As a general rule, you should avoid just throwing the list of observations under the heading. (**Note:** Use a colon at the end of the set-up to introduce the list that follows and connect it to the sentence.)

Recommendations

If all you find during your inspection are positive elements to report, then you really won't need this section, since you won't have any recommendations to make. If you do find problems, however, you should suggest ways they might be fixed.

The format of this section should parallel the *Observations* section. Set up the list of recommendations as you did the observations. The recommendations should be given *in the same order* as the problems observed. For example: If the first problem you mention is that there were no fire extinguishers in the building, then the first recommendation might be to install fire extinguishers in strategic locations throughout the building. For each bullet point listed under *Observations*, you should have a corresponding bullet point under *Recommendations*.

This may seem obvious, but students sometimes forget to include a recommendation for a problem observed. Worse, they often suggest ways to resolve problems that were never mentioned under *Observations*. Double-check your lists!

Closing

Your memo should end with a paragraph that invites the recipient to respond to the memo in some way. The closing can be as simple as:

If you have any questions, please call me at 555-5555 or contact me at acmebuilders.com.

If your firm does building repair work, however, the closing is a good time to solicit the work that needs to be done on the building in your report. Always keep the door open for future communications.

TRIP MEMO

Companies often send employees off-site, for a number of reasons. Perhaps the company has a project in another town and needs someone to go review the work done and submit a report on the progress being made. An important national conference may offer the opportunity for someone in the company to demonstrate its products or services; or an employee may present a program. The company may be thinking of expanding and send someone to a few locations to see which would best suit the company's needs and budget.

As you can see, the *purpose* of each of these reports is different. But they all involve an employee going somewhere other than the home office to investigate or observe and then reporting on what was investigated or observed to someone who did not make the trip. Whatever other category the report might fit into (e.g., a progress report), it is also a *trip report memo*.

The key to a good trip report, as in any business writing, is *focus*. Remember that the purpose of your report is to tell the recipient what you saw or experienced. How you got there, what you ate or what you did for fun in the evenings is totally irrelevant. What *is* relevant will depend on the reason behind your trip. If you are reviewing progress on a company project in another city, your focus would most likely be on how well the project is meeting expected time lines and other goals. If you are reporting on a conference, the focus would probably be on some key concepts gleaned from meetings and presentations. If you are scouting locations for expansion, the focus would center on how well the area visited matches your company's growth objectives.

The format of a trip report memo is the same as the format for an inspection report memo. The person receiving the memo might be your immediate supervisor or someone higher up. This is also a situation where you might send a copy of the memo to one or more people (the CC line comes immediately after the To line). Again, the Subject line is crucial. It must make clear to the recipient(s) what the memo is about.

First Paragraph

The opening paragraph of the trip memo should include the following:

- where you went;
- why you went; and
- when you went.

If you made the trip at the request of the recipient, it's a good idea to remind her of that (e.g., Last week you asked me to visit our site in Jacksonville and report on progress there). If you are participating in a convention, it would be helpful to provide a brief (one or two sentence) summary of the nature of the convention and its interest to your company.

Details Section

The next few paragraphs of the memo should summarize your observations/impressions from the trip. You want to be specific and provide concrete details, especially if you are reporting on progress made at a work site or the potential for a location to serve the company's expansion needs. Many companies have forms for progress reports. In that case, you would probably provide a brief written note on what you observed and attach the completed report form.

In this section, you may want to include graphs or tables to help illustrate what you are reporting. For example, if you have visited two or three sites for possible expansion, a table showing the sites' relative strengths and weaknesses would be helpful. Supporting details are important, but make sure the details are relevant to the *purpose* of your report.

Follow-Up Section

This particular section could have one of several titles as a heading. If your report contains observations of problems that need to be addressed, then you would need a *Recommendations* section following the details presented. If you or someone else corrected the problem, then the section would be called *Actions Taken* or something similar.

As always, be sure to end this memo with an invitation for further inquiry from the recipient.

RECOMMENDATION MEMO

The final memo is a recommendation memo. In it you will present your part of a team fact-finding project comparing similar products and recommending one for purchase. A recommendation report is used to present options for a superior or a client regarding possible choices for a product or service that the person or company needs. It involves researching and assessing the products to see if they meet the desired qualities. The report may result in a specific recommendation for one product, or it might offer options. The purpose is to make it easy for the person receiving the report to make a decision.

First, the team has to select a type of product (e.g., computers, cars, etc.). After that, you should:

- Decide how to narrow the field of possible products to compare.
- Determine which products to compare and how to divide the research.
- Narrow the points of comparison.
- Decide how to break up the information to be presented.

Normally, this selection would be made for you, as you would be responding to a specific request for information from your superior or client.

Select a type of product.

For the purposes of this assignment, the type of product being compared is less important than the care and planning that go into making the comparison and recommendation. Your team can choose almost any product, but it would be useful to make it something a business might actually need. That includes a variety of possibilities, from office products (computers, printers, scanners) to fleet vehicles (trucks or cars) to appliances for an employee lounge (microwaves, coffee makers, refrigerators).

Decide how to narrow the field of possible products to compare.

Any category of products will include many more choices, over a range of prices and capabilities, than would be practical or useful to compare. Your team needs to narrow the universe of products to be compared by establishing specific criteria for inclusion, depending on the products involved. Criteria for light trucks, for example, might include:

- price range;
- seating capacity; and
- four-wheel drive capability.

The idea is to make the comparison useful and reasonable. Comparing a $50,000 full-size truck to a $20,000 small truck might not be too helpful. The key point is to make clear to your reader how you decided to compare the particular products you discuss in your memo.

Determine which products to compare and how to divide the research.

After you have established the selection criteria, the team can begin research to find products that meet those criteria. From there it should be an easy step to assign research to each team member. One way would be to have each member research one product at this stage. The important point is to gather as much information as possible. That will help when the team compares notes for deciding how to break up the information for each person's memo.

Narrow the points of comparison.

Once the team has researched the information available on the products selected for comparison in the recommendation report, you need to decide the specific criteria on which the products will be compared. You will find a plethora of specs on any given product, so you have to decide which are the most important—or most relevant—to the use to which this product might be put. The average fuel efficiency of a small truck, for example, is probably more useful as a point of comparison than axle width.

The important point here is that *all* team members are presenting information on the same criteria. If fuel efficiency is an agreed upon criterion, then that information should be provided for all vehicles in the report.

Decide how to break up information to be presented.

The individual memos can be organized in different ways. Your team may decide to have each person take one product and report on it, or have team members take particular categories of comparison for *all* products being compared. An advantage to this pattern is that it makes a more logical comparison, as opposed to just listing specs for one product.

# Formal Reports

A formal report contains several sections. It is usually bound in most business communications. The following provides some guidance on the various parts of a formal business report:

1. Letter of Transmittal
2. Cover Page
3. Table of Contents
4. Executive Summary
5. Body of Report
6. Bibliography and Appendices (if needed).

If the report is to be bound, you will need to use a wider left margin (2") so the text won't fall into the gutter of the page. Otherwise, you can generally use the default margins for a word processing program. As for business memos, you should use a clean 12-point font (Times New Roman, Arial, etc.) and single space, with double spacing between paragraphs and headings.

There may be a great deal of repetition in the report, since you will need to include the same information in several sections of the report. For example, the Executive Summary can literally be put together by some judicious copying and pasting, with perhaps a little re-tooling to fit the nature of the Executive Summary. (**Note:** Be very careful, however, *not* to do a cut-and-paste. Otherwise, you might leave some serious gaps in the report. Proofreading carefully should help discover any of these accidents.)

The style for the report should be standard business writing. Avoid slang and contractions, for example. But use the same economy of style that you employ in a memo. Make your point, support it as needed—and move on. The goal of a formal business report is still to convey information in a straightforward manner.

You still need to consider your readers and their likely level of familiarity with the subject at hand. If you are comparing products to suggest one for purchase, for instance, you might not need more than a cursory explanation of the product's purpose and use. If, on the other hand, you are explaining a new manufacturing process, a more detailed explanation might be required.

The parts of the report outlined below each have a purpose. (As you will see, it is much like the recommendation memo, at least in the case given below, only longer and more developed.) Any formal report should include each section. The only exceptions would be the Bibliography, if you aren't using outside sources, and the Appendices.

1. Letter of Transmittal

A letter of transmittal is exactly what is sounds like: a letter *transmitting* a report from you to the person who is receiving it. It should use a standard business letter format and is usually paper-clipped to the outside of the bound report.

The letter should be relatively brief and to the point. Basically, what you are saying is, "Here's a report on X" or "Attached is the report/information you requested." You should include a short paragraph on the subject of the report and, in some cases, a short summary of the conclusions reached in the report.

The letter of transmittal could also be a *memo* of transmittal, especially if the report is an internal project. Just use a standard business memo format and, again, attach the memo to the outside of the report.

A sample letter of transmittal follows:

2512 Exeter Road
Tampa, Florida 33612
August 25, 2002

Arnold Smithers, CEO
Southern States Delivery
115 South Bend Road
Gainesville, Florida 35676

Dear Mr. Smithers:

Attached is our report on the environmental status of the property at 1151 Orange Grove Lane that your company is considering buying. As you requested, we did a thorough investigation of environmental conditions and issues for the property.

Based on our preliminary findings, we recommend that Southern States Delivery *not* purchase the property—unless several serious problems are corrected first. You will note in the report at least five situations for which the EPA has cited the current property owners. We have included details on those and other concerns in the report.

Please feel free to call me if you have any questions.

Sincerely,

Doug Crane, Vice President
Environmental Services

Figure 2: Sample Letter of Transmittal

2. Cover Page

The first part of the report itself is the cover page. The cover page should include:

- the title of the report;
- your name and your company's name; and
- the date the report is submitted.

For class purposes you would include the course and section number and your instructor's name.

Environmental Impact Study:
1151 Orange Grove Lane
Prepared for Southern States Delivery

Doug Crane, Vice President
Environmental Services
Tampa Consulting, Inc.
August 25, 2002

Figure 3: Sample Cover Page

3. Table of Contents

Even a relatively brief report can benefit from a Table of Contents. It serves as a handy reference point for the reader to find a specific bit of information, without having to work through the entire report.

Most word processing programs will generate a Table of Contents automatically, although it takes a bit of preparation. You will need to check the program's instructions to see how to tell it how to group the sections of your report by level—i.e., main point, sub-section and so on. It's worth the early effort. You don't want to spend more time creating a Table of Contents than you do writing the report itself.

Most Tables of Contents list the topic/heading flush left, with the beginning page number for each topic/heading set flush right. The two are connected by a series of spaced periods. Trying to insert those periods by hand can become quite difficult, since letters and numbers each require a slightly different amount of space. An "H," for example, requires less space than an "I." The difference may be hard to detect by the naked eye, but it is there. The programs' Table of Contents generators automatically adjust individual spacing to make everything align.

4. Executive Summary

An executive summary is just what the name implies—literally, a summary (of the report and its findings) for the "executive" to whom the report is sent. Its main purpose is to provide a brief, but thorough overview of the information and recommendations contained in the report for someone who does not have the time (or does not need to take the time) to read the whole report.

The length of an executive summary depends on the length and complexity of the report. A good rule of thumb is that an executive summary should be no more than one-tenth the length of the report. A report that is 10 pages or less would generally need an executive summary that is one page or less. A 30-page report might need an executive summary of up to three pages.

In the executive summary you should include a brief statement about the subject matter and purpose of the report, a summary of the main points of investigation and discovery and a listing of the key conclusions or recommendations.

You should use headings in the executive summary that correspond to the headings in the report, e.g., "Summary of Findings" and "Recommendations." The initial paragraph of the executive summary should establish what the report concerns and, if relevant, how the information was obtained, i.e., through primary sources (information you generated yourself through interviews or experiments) or secondary sources (journal articles and Internet sites).

For the most part, you should be able to do a "copy and paste" from the report itself for the bulk of the executive summary. (Remember: Be very careful not to execute a "cut and paste" instead. You don't want to leave any puzzling gaps in the report.) Some sections may have to be rephrased slightly to work in the executive summary, but most will not.

Don't worry about repetition, here or in the body of the report. Some information *needs* to be repeated in different sections, in case the reader only wants to read one part of the report.

5. Body of Report

The body of the report has several sections:

- An introductory paragraph or two
- Purpose
- Scope of the Study
- Research Methods
- Findings
- Summary of Findings
- Conclusions and Recommendations.

For simplicity's sake, let's assume this report will be a product recommendation report, in which you compare three or more similar products (e.g., sport utility vehicles) and recommend one for purchase. (Actually, a recommendation report may *not* conclude that one company's product is clearly superior to others; the final recommendation may offer several alternatives to the reader.)

Introduction. You need to begin by introducing the nature/subject of the report and provide any appropriate background information. Remember to keep focused, here and throughout the report. If you are comparing sport utility vehicles (SUVs), for example, a background section might include comments on the rapid increase of SUVs in the American market over the last 10 years and some statistics on what percentage of automobile sales SUVs make up in the United States. You don't need to talk about America's love affair with cars in general or trace the origin of transportation from the first wheel to today's SUV.

Purpose. Here you would indicate why you researched this subject and the intended audience for your report (e.g., a middle-class family looking for a larger vehicle).

Scope of the Study. In this section you need to indicate how you narrowed the selection of products to be compared. Price might be a factor, for instance, as might certain safety features that are deemed essential.

The point is, you need to focus on a particular subset of SUVs, and not compare a $60,000 vehicle to a $30,000 one. To be meaningful, the comparison has to have a logical base. In this section, you would name the three or more vehicles that meet the criteria for selection to be included in your comparison.

Research Methods. You need to make clear how you found the information that serves as the basis for your comparison. (It shouldn't just be your personal knowledge and opinion.) Did you consult car or consumer magazines, either online or in "hard copy"? Did you interview salesmen and/or owners of SUVs for their evaluations? The first would be *secondary* resources, i.e., information you gleaned from an existing source. The second would be *primary* resources, information you gathered first-hand. Both can be valuable.

Findings. Here you establish the five or six points on which your comparison was made (e.g., price, warranty, safety, resale value, fuel efficiency, etc.). Include a sub-heading for each point, and present the information found. Usually, it's best to organize the results from best to worst in each category (e.g., the least expensive, the mid-range expensive and the most expensive SUV, within the price range established for selection). You might want to include charts or graphs to add to the presentation of data. Some people grasp information more easily from a chart or graph than from a narrative sentence. Others are the opposite. It's always a good idea to present both, where appropriate and possible.

Summary of Findings. This is where you present the main points you made for each of the categories of comparison. You need to re-state the categories of comparison *and* the products compared at the start of this section. (See how repetition creeps in. The point is, someone might only want to read the Summary of Findings section and skip the rest of the report.) It would be helpful to have a separate bullet paragraph for each category, with the subject (e.g., **Cost**) boldfaced for ease of location. You don't need to repeat all of what you reported in the previous section—just the highlights.

Conclusions and Recommendations. Here you will want to report the basic conclusions reached for each category of comparison. (Repetition again, although the information is a little more specific and focused.) And this is where you present your recommendation(s) to the reader. As noted earlier, you may find one product is clearly superior to the others and should be recommended. But you might also discover that one product can be recommended for one person (e.g., someone for whom price is the ultimate concern), and a second product can be recommended for someone else (e.g., a person who is most interested in safety). It is also conceivable that you might conclude that *none* of the products can be recommended over the others. That is also a legitimate conclusion to reach.

6. Bibliography and Appendices

If you used outside resources for your report, you need to list them in a bibliography. You can list them all together or by category (e.g., Interviews and Articles). In either case, create your bibliography by putting your sources in alphabetical order (last name first). Then number each source consecutively. This holds even if you have two different categories. If the last entry under Interviews is number 4, then the first entry under the next category (e.g., Articles) would be number 5. The reason: You can use the *numbers* of the entries to provide attribution for information in your report, so you do not want two number 1s. (Consult a research style manual for the format of Bibliography entries, including Internet sources.)

Appendices are good locations for information that doesn't fit neatly into your report, but that adds to the value of the report. This might be a place to locate charts and graphs or to present related information gathered during your research (e.g., a more complete safety study for the vehicles).

5

Giving a Professional Oral Presentation

Many people have a fear of public speaking ... but there are better solutions.

PROFESSIONALLY SPEAKING

You already know from Chapter Four that you will be responsible for doing a lot of writing as an engineer, writing that is often more business than science in nature. But another responsibility you may find handed to you in your job is making oral presentations. These might include:

- a brief summary of your team's project to the rest of your department;
- a presentation at a professional meeting to outline your company's new building process; or
- a pitch to the City Council concerning your firm's plans for the new bridge project the council is funding.

DILBERT reprinted by permission of United Feature Syndicate, Inc.

The audience may change; the purpose may be different. But, in the end, a good speech is like good music—if it works well and is understandable, it will be successful and appreciated.

You may be one of those people Dogbert is referring to above who fear public speaking more than a trip to the dentist. Chances are, however, you *will* be called upon to speak during the course of your professional career. The best defense against the uneasiness brought on by standing up before a group of people to talk is to be prepared. The more work you do ahead of time, the better you should feel. You may never come to love speaking in public, but you can learn to approach it with something like confidence—as opposed to dread.

This chapter is designed to give you some tips for researching, organizing and preparing a professional speech. These are common sense steps, but you know the saying about how uncommon "common sense" is. Most of you have probably given speeches, either in high school or in other college courses, and some of what you read here will echo previous learning. But you may have forgotten some of these tips. If you have never spoken in public before, however, these ideas will help you do a better job. The keys to any good speech are preparation, perseverance—and practice. Lots of practice.

Preparation Saves

Students hate to do research. They abhor taking notes. They detest taking time to prepare an outline to organize their thoughts. And they would rather "wing it" than actually practice—out loud, for goodness sake—the speech they intend to give.

But now we're talking about professional responsibility: doing the work that is expected of you in order to represent your department or your company out in the world. So now is the time to begin dedicating yourself to an organized approach to speaking in public. It really isn't so bad. Honest.

The "research" required for any given topic will vary. The first oral project in this text, for example, is a report on a building inspection, to be done by the company your team formed earlier. So the research you will do for that presentation will be visual in nature. You might need to dig (not literally, please) to find some historic information about the building, but the bulk of what you will say will be based on your first-hand observation of the building itself. (By the way, the first presentation is a group one for a purpose: Those of you who are unsure about speaking in public should feel a little better, at least, surrounded by teammates for moral support.)

For the second presentation, a set of instructions, you might have to do some research to find background information on your topic. On the other hand, if the presentation is based on some hobby you have, then your own experience and knowledge base will provide the material you need to prepare the talk.

The final presentation, however, will require some research. It is a product comparison report—done as a team, again—comparing similar products and recommending the best one. The research you do will vary. You may gather information from many sources:

- magazine articles;
- internet sources;
- interviews with sales representatives; or
- testing the products yourself.

The key will be to find enough information to make an *informed* recommendation.

(**Note:** Each of the three oral presentations has a corresponding *written* assignment, as outlined in the previous chapter. The final products will be slightly different, but you will be able to use the same information in both.)

Organization vs. Chaos

Once you have gathered the information you need, whether through observation or research, you need to organize it. Remember, you are the one who knows what information you intend to convey to your listener. You may have a firm grasp of that information. But you have to present it to your audience in a way they can understand and follow. Otherwise, your point can be lost.

Before you can organize your material, you must consider some key questions:

- What is the *purpose* of your talk? Are you trying to persuade someone to a particular point of view? Or are you mainly trying to inform your audience?
- How much *time* do you have to present? You can cover much more ground, obviously, in a 20-minute talk than you can in a 10-minute talk.
- How informed is your *audience* about the topic at hand? Do you need to introduce background information or define terms?

Other questions will arise, but these three sets are crucial. They will help you establish the nature of the information you need to present, as well as the best style with which to present it.

Purpose

For most of the situations in which you are speaking as a professional engineer, your purpose will be mainly to inform:

- filling in your department on the progress of a major project you are directing;
- speaking at a professional meeting about a new chip your company is developing; or
- explaining a complex process to potential investors.

In other situations, however, you may be trying to persuade your audience, such as:

- telling a company planning committee why your project should get top funding priority;
- selling your company to a city council as the best one to complete the new park project—on time and under budget; or
- convincing a potential client that you and your company are best suited to meet their needs.

The *purpose* of your talk, then, is a critical component in your planning process. You can use the same information in several ways. The important point is to decide which approach best meets the purpose that puts you in front of the audience in the first place.

Time

In many instances, you will be given a set amount of time in which to make your presentation. It might be 10 minutes or 20 minutes or an hour. You want to use your time as wisely and effectively as possible. Think of the possible information you can present on a given topic as a pie: The more time you have, the bigger the slice of information you can cover.

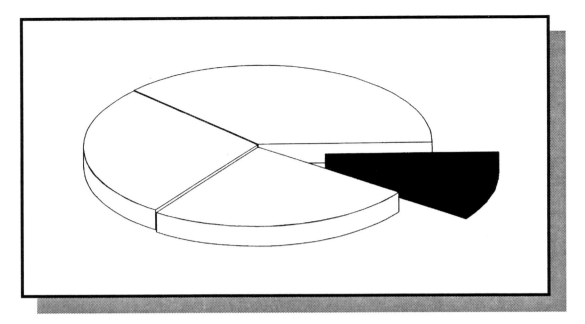

Figure 1: A Slice of Time

Audience

Another variable involved in deciding how much detail to give in your presentation is the audience who will be hearing it. In some cases, your audience will be very familiar with the concepts presented and terminology used; in other cases, they may be completely baffled if you give them too much detail or use esoteric terms.

If you are making a pitch to a government body to sell them on your firm as the right one to hire for a project, you have to give them the information in terms they can understand. Most city councils, for example, are composed of educated men and women—but few, if any, are likely to be engineers or scientists. That means you have to explain some ideas in a non-scientific way. You never want to talk down to an audience, but you also don't want to leave them baffled.

What this means in terms of planning and organizing your presentation is that you will need to factor in time—and perhaps graphics and other visual support—to clarify your presentation for laymen.

Another tip: Try to connect with your audience in informal ways. If you know, for example, that several of the city council members are avid golfers, perhaps you can build in a few allusions to golfing as you explain your project: "You'll find our company is long off the tee and has a great approach shot as we close in on a project." Be careful, though. Make sure you are using such references correctly. The backfire for a sporting or other faux pas can be deadly.

Researching—On the Job

On the job, most of the research you will be doing will involve the actual planning for the project you will be presenting. In other words, *you*—and your team, if one is involved—will be one of your key resources. But you may also need to gather information from other departments in your company, or examine the details of similar projects.

It helps to have a fairly clear idea of what it is you are researching. That may change over time, as you fine tune your approach, but you do need a starting point. You need to be familiar with sources of information. You should have some experience already with using a library and the Internet for research. On the job, you might find information in many places—and in many forms.

If your company has done similar projects, it's always a good idea to look at the documents for those projects. This can help in a number of ways. For one thing, you may find some background material on your company that you can simply import into your own presentation. No need to reinvent the wheel. For another, you will become familiar with the accepted language used within your company. Some companies and organizations develop a specific way of saying something: key words to be used; certain phrases to be included; and, equally important, words and phrases to *avoid* using. Using wording that has been used previously in company documents and speeches is *not* plagiarism. It is simply maintaining a style, a pattern of usage, within the company.

If you are preparing a presentation in response to a Request for Proposals (RFP), it is always a good idea to echo the language used in the RFP in your presentation. Reviewers will respond to familiar phrasing. In fact, if the RFP specifically requests that you address A, B and C, then your effort will suffer if A, B and C aren't clearly addressed. The key to any effective communication, remember, is to make it as easy as possible for the reader/audience to follow you. What better guideposts to use than the ones the "audience" itself provides?

There is another rich source of information in most companies, too: people. Every company has at least one person who has "been there, done that." Often such employees become the unofficial historians of the organization. It's a good idea to search out such truffles and cultivate them. You may be rewarded with some important insights or shortcuts to finding information you need.

Researching—For Class

Finding resources for your class presentations should be a familiar task. You will use the same resources you have been using throughout your educational experience—with one exception, which I will address shortly. You will need to consult the standard library resources, of course, as well as sources on the Internet. A balance would be useful in most cases, since there are advantages and disadvantages to both published and Internet resources.

Information that has been published—especially in book form—is, by its nature, "old." That means it could be too dated on ever-changing topics such as computers. On the other hand, one advantage of published information is that is has been tested and screened for accuracy in most cases, either by reviewers or by editors—or both. Material that appears in scholarly journals, as opposed to popular magazines, has generally been reviewed by other scholars before it is published. The key decision for published material, then, is whether it is current enough to be useful.

Information on the Internet, on the other hand, is usually quite current. It can be updated daily, or even more frequently. So Internet resources have the advantage of being up-to-date, generally reflecting the most recent thinking on the topic. But that immediacy can also be a disadvantage. Information can be posted without thorough review. Consider, for example, the information nightmare of the 2000 presidential election, when winners became losers—and then winners again. Instant information can often be wrong, whether on purpose or because of the need to be "first" with a story or theory. One important decision you need to make as a researcher regarding Internet information is whether that information is reliable. One solution is to do what reporters are taught to do: Get the information from more than one source.

A related problem in using Internet sources is the anonymity of much of what is posted on the Web. A researcher has no real way of knowing whether someone whose opinion is posted on a Web site named "Ford Stinks," for example, is a reasonably knowledgeable adult or a 10-year old kid. Sticking to corporate Web sites or legitimate consumer Web sites, as opposed to chat rooms or opinion sites, might be a good idea. At least weigh the source of the information carefully if you use it.

> # Assignment 1: Building Inspection
>
> The first team class assignment is to do an oral report on an inspection of a campus building. (This assignment is coordinated with a written assignment explained in Chapter Four.) The report will be delivered by the company you have formed with your team in an earlier assignment. There are several steps involved in this assignment:
>
> 1. Choose a building to inspect.
> 2. Decide on areas of concern to be addressed in the inspection.
> 3. Divide the inspection into parts for each team member.
> 4. Create individual segments in PowerPoint format.
> 5. Unify individual segments into a coherent PowerPoint presentation.
>
> This assignment will take some team effort, as well as individual work. It is essential that each member of the team contribute to the process, and class attendance is an important part of that effort. If you haven't already done so, team members should be sure to exchange contact information (e.g., e-mail addresses and phone numbers). That way you can stay in contact with your group and its progress if you have to miss class for some reason.

1. Choose a building to inspect.

Each team/company is to select a building on campus to inspect. (Selection is limited to campus buildings to facilitate the inspection process during class time.) There can be no duplication of buildings selected in a class section. A few ideas to consider:

- Older buildings might have more problems to report on than newer buildings.
- Newer buildings, on the other hand, may provide more to comment on regarding meeting code requirements and aesthetic qualities.
- Since at least part of your inspection will take place during class time, some areas of buildings might be off limits because of classes in session.

2. Decide on areas of concern to be addressed in the inspection.

This is not to be a thorough structural inspection such as a firm might do under real circumstances. You won't need to dig up the foundation to search for faults or pop ceiling tiles to inspect electrical conduits or water pipes. But you should observe obvious signs of damage, such as stress cracks in walls, water stains on ceiling tiles or badly worn stairs.

Several areas of concern can be inspected in any building; specialized buildings such as recreational centers or labs have additional issues to consider. Major issues to consider might include:

- General safety
  - Easily identified emergency exits
  - Clean and uncluttered hallways
  - Stairways clearly marked and passable
  - No-slip outside stairs

- Fire safety
  - Fire alarms visible and marked
  - Emergency lights
  - Fire exits clearly marked
  - Extinguishers available and charged

- Accessibility
  - Ramps leading into the building
  - Electronic door openers
  - Bathrooms accessible
  - Access to floors available for those in wheelchairs

- Aesthetics
  - Condition and appeal of building exterior
  - Condition and appeal of grounds around building
  - Interior conditions (e.g., colors used)
  - General atmosphere of building.

These are only some of the points your team may want to consider during the inspection. If your building includes labs, then lab safety would be an important consideration (e.g., eye wash stations, emergency showers, ventilation). The key is to make the inspection together as a team, take notes and then compare notes later. Having several sets of eyes considering the complete inspection at the beginning can prove helpful later, when specific details need to be generated.

3. Divide the inspection into parts for each team member.

Once your team has made the inspection, you need to decide how to divide up the oral presentation of your report. One way to do that is for each person to take one aspect of the inspection (e.g., general safety or access). Another way would be to do a floor by floor report, where practical. (That can get a little clumsy, however.) For major sections such as fire safety or access, two members of the team could split the report. It is difficult to give precise guidelines, since each building will offer different areas of consideration.

Please don't feel limited to only negative observations. A report can be positive in nature as well. If a building meets fire safety requirements, it is certainly permissible to give it a positive report in that area.

If you do report negative conditions, however, be prepared to offer recommendations for improving the problems you find. Since this is an exercise, you will not be responsible for carrying out those recommendations, of course. But they should be practical and achievable, given the money to carry them out. In other words, razing the building and starting from scratch will probably *not* be workable options, as noted earlier.

(**Note:** The recommendation section will be an important part of your written assignment related to the building inspection in Chapter Four.)

4. Create individual segments in PowerPoint format.

Once team members have developed their area of the presentation, each member can create a set of PowerPoint slides. The team needs to decide on which background, font and style to use for the slides so that the next step goes smoothly.

Selecting the background should be relatively simple, and PowerPoint allows you to change the background on slides easily. Other points to consider for unity of appearance in the slides include:

- font style, color and size for headlines and text;
- use of animation available in the program;
- style and format of lists; and
- use of photos.

Generally, you want to make the type as shown on a monitor or projected on a screen easy to read. Use a 24-point font or larger for headlines, for example, and at least an 18-point font for text. The color of your type should not bleed into the background color of your slides or clash in a way that makes your audience avert their eyes in pain. (Believe me, it can happen.)

PowerPoint offers a variety of ways to animate the text on your slides and allows you to import animated figures. A word of advice: Don't get carried away. Less is definitely better in a professional business presentation. Be consistent in how you get your text to appear (e.g., sliding in from the left or right). Be sure to check for the sound effects that accompany the animation as well. They can be quite annoying and may cause your audience to riot. Shutting off the sound might be very wise.

As you generate lists in your presentation, you and your teammates should have an agreement on the style and format of those lists. The idea is to create a uniform group presentation. Will you use bullets or numbered lists? Will you use phrases or sentences for the items in your lists? (Each list must be internally parallel in form—all sentences or all words/phrases.) Some variety is permitted, of course, but you don't want your presentation to look like a Frankenstein's monster of patched together parts. Strive to make it seamless.

Some teams like to take digital pictures of the building they inspect and import those pictures into their PowerPoint slides. Photos can add a dramatic impact to your presentation. They can underscore specific points made (e.g., cracks in flooring or stains on ceiling tiles). The only downside to adding photos to your presentation is that they can take up a great deal of space, more than a 3.5" floppy disk can accommodate. Your team can work around that by burning the presentation on a CD. (If the class is held in a computer lab, the file can be saved on someone's university account space and transferred into the instructor's computer for display.) It's not a good idea to disrupt the flow of your presentation by swapping floppies as you go.

A final note about creating your slides: Don't try to put too much information on any one slide. Two or three bullet points per slide can be quite legible. Ten can be impossible to read. Unlike the old 2 × 2 slides, PowerPoint slides do not cost money to generate (unless you print them). If your presentation contains 40 slides instead of 10, the quality of your talk will not be affected. It *will* be affected, however, if your slides are too packed to read.

5. Unify individual segments into a coherent PowerPoint presentation.

After all the individual parts of the presentation are finished, one member of the team needs to integrate them into one coherent PowerPoint presentation. This is the time to make sure the backgrounds and styles are all alike. Each person is responsible for the grammar and usage on his or her slides. It's always a good idea for all team members to check the entire presentation for any problems. As with any other form of professional communication, grammatical errors, spelling flubs and typos can detract from your presentation. PROOFREAD CAREFULLY.

Timing the Presentation

The team needs to practice the presentation for timing purposes. Your team's presentation should take between 15 and 20 minutes, as a rule. The only true way to measure the time required to "speak" a presentation is to practice it aloud. There are guidelines for the time required to deliver a speech (e.g., roughly five minutes per typed, single-spaced page), but those are only guides. Each person has a different pace of delivery. And the time it takes to speak a page is *not* the same as the time it takes to read it silently.

Each student should practice speaking his or her presentation to get individual timing down. The team also needs to practice together. Transitions from one speaker to the next should be smooth. That doesn't have to be much more than, "Now Jennifer will report on general safety issues." But you don't want to leave a teammate hanging. Think of it as a relay race in track. You are handing the baton off to the next speaker. Make it smooth—and don't drop it.

ASSIGNMENT TWO: INSTRUCTIONS

Each student is to select a topic on which to present instructions. This is a relatively open assignment—within reason. You may choose to present instructions on how to make something or how to complete a specific task. If you have a hobby, that might serve as a workable topic for you. Aim for 10-15 minutes. Steps to consider in this assignment:

1. Select the topic.
2. Consider the audience's likely familiarity with the topic.
3. Organize carefully.
4. Decide where to place warnings.
5. Decide on method of presentation.
6. Practice, practice, practice.

---

1. Select the topic.

Give some thought to selecting your topic. The idea of having this assignment is that people are more comfortable speaking about a topic in which they are very interested and about which they know a great deal. When you make a speech as a professional, you will most likely be presenting information that you have created or researched yourself. Having a good handle on the information used should help reduce the tension you might feel about speaking in public.

The topic itself can vary widely. One excellent model for a set of instructions is a recipe. The structure and content of a recipe are clear—and very exact. All the information a person needs to prepare the recipe is there:

- ingredients needed (and in what quantity);
- equipment needed (e.g., mixer, measuring spoons);
- specific preparation information (e.g., temperature and time for cooking); and
- step-by-step instructions for preparation.

(**Note:** In order to make a recipe presentation long enough, consider adding interesting background information. For example, does this recipe have significance within your family or culture? Have you had problems making it? Anecdotal information that might not work in a written set of instructions can add a nice flair to an oral presentation.)

If you are giving instructions on how to build a deck onto a house, the same pattern applies:

- supplies instead of ingredients (e.g., type and size of lumber needed, screws);
- tools instead of equipment (e.g., level, saw);
- specific preparation information (e.g., preparing the wood for the decking); and
- the step-by-step instructions for building the deck.

The same model can apply for how to play a sport, how to make a musical instrument or how to build an airplane.

Computers offer a variety of possible topics, from how to install a piece of hardware to how to construct a Web page.

2. Consider the audience's likely familiarity with the topic.

As with any presentation, you must consider the audience you are addressing and their understanding of the topic. For our purposes, your audience will be your classmates, and you can assume they would know what the "average" college student would know about your topic. You don't want to speak over your audience's head, but you also don't want to insult their intelligence.

It's always a good practice to present the parameters of understanding that you have used to create your presentation. You can assume, for example, that college students know what a computer is. And engineering students should have more than a passing knowledge of computers. But all your classmates are not going to be computer science majors or programmers. A good way to be sure of what level of understanding your audience is comfortable with—on any topic—is to ask (e.g., "Does everyone know what X is?"). This is not as formal a presentation as others might be. It can be more conversational and can include a demonstration as well.

If your topic is very specialized, you might want to begin by defining some terms or key concepts being used. A handout explaining terms and concepts might be useful, as well.

3. Organize carefully.

Organization is a key element in an instructions talk. Steps must be clearly defined and should be in a logical sequence. Nothing interrupts the flow of a talk as much as having to say, "Oh, yes, remember step 2? I should have mentioned that the battery might explode if you don't wire it properly." (See step 4 below.)

In addition to warnings, however, you must also consider how to organize the *steps* of your process logically. Think about the instructions you have read (more likely ignored) over the years. The sequence of steps should follow one from the other. In installing a piece of computer hardware, for example, you have to remove the PC cover *before* you find the location bay for the drive being installed. It's a simple concept, but one that people often forget—especially when instructing someone else on a task they have done many times.

A helpful way to approach putting instructions together, whether oral or written, is to try to imagine what someone who has never done this before needs to know to get started. How did you approach doing it the first time? Being very familiar with a topic can be useful, but it can also make it more difficult to see the project from a newcomer's perspective. One good way to check on whether your instructions are logical and easy to follow is to have someone read them—or listen to them.

4. Decide where to place warnings.

Many instructions have warnings of different magnitude included, from simple notes to warnings of danger. Sometimes they come at the beginning of the instructions; more often, however, they occur within the instructions themselves. The key concept to follow is that any warning should come *BEFORE* the step involved. That may seem simple and obvious, but you will find instructions, even professionally prepared ones, that don't follow that guideline.

Sometimes such placement is a matter of convenience; sometimes it is vitally important. Overall warnings about approaching a project should clearly come at the beginning on the instructions. Often that takes shape as a note:

(**Note:** Be sure to ground yourself before opening the computer casing.)

But warnings about specific steps need to be placed just before that step:

Warning: Be sure to block the opposite tires before jacking up your car.

There are various levels of warnings possible:

- A **Note** generally is used to convey information that is interesting or important, but not a step as such.
- A **Caution** warns of possible problems involved with a step if not done properly.
- A **Warning** usually notes possible damage to equipment or the validity of the process in the step following.
- A **Danger** is used to convey the possibility of serious damage or possible harm to the person doing the project. The last is used sparingly and reserved for inherently dangerous tasks, such as refueling a plane or cleaning a blast furnace.

Picking the level of warning is up to you. (Recipes hardly ever call for "Warnings" or "Dangers" unless, of course, you are describing the preparation of a flaming dessert.) Just be sure to properly prepare your audience if there might be problems.

5. Decide on method of presentation.

The method of presentation you use in this assignment will depend on the nature of your topic. It might be a PowerPoint show, a demonstration or a combination of both. If you present a talk on building a deck on a home, it would obviously be difficult to do a demonstration in a classroom. For those subjects, a PowerPoint demonstration would probably work best. Discussing how to install a video card, on the other hand, could be done as a demonstration in class. And presenting a recipe might use a combination of PowerPoint slides and demonstration (no cooking in class, of course).

If you use a combination of methods, you should be sure to practice sufficiently so the presentation is as smooth as possible. Shifting from one method to another can be quite tricky and distracting.

6. Practice, practice, practice (Part 2).

As with any presentation, the key to making this instruction presentation work is practice. This is a fairly informal presentation, but you want it to be smooth and natural. The idea is to pick a topic that is familiar to you so you will be comfortable. Even so, it is necessary to practice for timing, if nothing else.

This is meant to be an enjoyable assignment, so choose your topic wisely. Don't wait until the last minute and grab your grandmother's cornbread recipe.

ASSIGNMENT THREE: RECOMMENDATION REPORT

This is another team project. Each team will create a PowerPoint presentation to recommend which of several products a consumer should buy. The team must:

1. Select a type of product (e.g., computers, cars, etc.).
2. Decide how to narrow the field of possible products to compare.
3. Determine which products to compare and how to divide the research.
4. Narrow the points of comparison.
5. Create individual PowerPoint segments.
6. Merge segments into a comprehensive whole.

A recommendation report is used to present options for a superior or a client regarding possible choices for a product or service that the person or company needs. It involves researching and assessing the products to see if they meet the desired qualities. The report may result in a specific recommendation for one product, or it might offer options. The purpose is to make it easy for the person receiving the report to make a decision.

1. Select a type of product (e.g., computers, cars, etc.).

For the purposes of this assignment, the type of product being compared is less important than the care and planning that go into making the comparison and recommendation. Your team can choose almost any product, but it would be useful to make it something a business might actually need. That includes a variety of possibilities, from office products (computers, printers, scanners) to fleet vehicles (trucks or cars) to appliances for an employee lounge (microwaves, coffee makers, refrigerators).

2. Decide how to narrow the field of possible products to compare.

Any category of products will include many more choices, over a range of prices and capabilities, than would be practical or useful to compare. Your team needs to narrow the universe of products to be compared by establishing specific criteria for inclusion, depending on the products involved. Criteria for light trucks, for example, might include:

- price range,
- seating capacity and
- four-wheel drive capability.

The idea is to make the comparison useful and reasonable. Comparing a $50,000 full-size truck to a $20,000 light truck might not be too helpful. The key point is to make clear to your audience how you decided to compare the particular product you discuss in your presentation.

3. Determine which products to compare and how to divide the research.

After you have established the selection criteria, the team can begin research to find products that meet those criteria. From there it should be an easy step to assign research to each team member. The easiest way would be to have each member research one product at this stage. The important point is to gather as much information as possible. That will help when the team compares notes for step 4.

4. Narrow the points of comparison.

Once the team has researched the information available on the products selected for comparison in the recommendation report, you need to decide the specific criteria on which the products will be compared. You will find a plethora of specs on any given product, so you have to decide which are the most important—or most relevant—for the use to which this product might be put. The average fuel efficiency of a small truck, for example, is probably more useful as a point of comparison than axle width.

The important point here is that *all* team members are presenting information on the same criteria. If fuel efficiency is an agreed upon criterion, then that information should be provided for all vehicles in the report.

5. Create individual PowerPoint segments.

Just as you did in the first team presentation, you should agree upon a background style, font and organizational scheme for individual segments of the team PowerPoint presentation.

The team presentation can be organized in different ways. You may decide to have each person take one product and report on it, then have a team member provide a recommendation summary. If you use this approach, be sure each presentation uses the same order of categories (e.g., price, warranty, fuel efficiency, cargo capacity and resale value). Otherwise, the team presentation will seem ragged and uncoordinated.

Another alternative is to have each team member report on all products being compared in two or three of the categories being used. An advantage to this pattern is that it makes it easier for the audience to follow over all. A careful building of slides will help as well.

Remember, the goal is to enable the audience to follow your presentation easily.

6. Merge segments into a comprehensive whole.

This step, again, will probably require that one person on the team assume responsibility for assembling the individual segments into a coherent whole. Each team member, however, should be involved in proofreading the presentation slides for technical errors and overall coherence.

Be sure to practice and time yourselves.

A Final Note

As mentioned earlier in this chapter, each of these oral presentations is paralleled by a writing assignment. (The previous chapter discussed the specifics of those assignments.) Although the technical requirements are different for an oral report and a written one, the basic information needed for one will serve the needs of the other. Good preparation for these oral presentations, then, will serve you well in preparing the written assignments.

6

Grammar and Usage

This chapter has been compiled to provide a quick reference tool for writing. It is not meant to be exhaustive, although it attempts to address common problems people face in their business writing. Various sources were consulted in putting this manual together. In those circumstances in which the sources disagree, one approach was generally chosen, instead of confusing the issue with options. The key to good writing is, first and foremost, consistency.

Topics include capitalization, punctuation, style and usage, writing style and English as a second language. Specific points are included in alphabetical order under each topic heading.

A few pearls of wisdom concerning style:

> "Our life is frittered away with detail ... Simplify, simplify."
>
> —Henry David Thoreau

> "Since writing is communication, clarity can only be a virtue."
>
> —Strunk and White

DILBERT reprinted by permission of United Feature Syndicate, Inc.

Capitalization

Government organizations

- Capitalize the official names of government organizations and institutions:

    U.S. Congress; Congress; the Senate; the House
    U.S. Supreme Court; the Supreme Court; the Court
    Department of Health and Human Services

- Use lower case for second references:

    The department; the agency

(**Note:** Congress, Senate and House are always capitalized.)

- Capitalize the title of a Member of Congress when used with the name of the member, but not when it stands alone:

    Sen. Edward M. Kennedy spoke to the members.
    The senator was quite supportive.

- Do not capitalize:

    cabinet; executive, legislative or judicial branch; federal

(**Note:** "Administration" is capitalized when it clearly refers to a specific administration—e.g., the Bush Administration, the Administration.)

Titles

- Formal titles directly preceding a person's name are capitalized:

    Chairman Frank Smith of Vital Inc. asked us for this report.

- Titles are not capitalized when they follow the person's name:

    Carl Johnson, president of the company, objected to the plan.

- Do not capitalize unofficial or occupational titles:

    researcher John Bloom; chemist Linus Pauling

- Capitalize "President" when referring to the President of the United States, but do not capitalize "presidential."

Punctuation

Punctuation is a road map that helps the reader understand what you have written. If punctuation confuses the reader, it's not doing its job.

Apostrophe

- Use an apostrophe to form the singular possessive, *but not the plural*, of abbreviations and acronyms ending in a capital letter:

    The HMO's director refused to comment.
    Many see HMOs as the answer to controlling costs.

- Do not use an apostrophe to form the plural of years, numbers or letters used as words:

    the 1960s; in twos and threes; the three Rs

- Apostrophes used with possessives:

    Plural nouns not ending in s: Add 's—the alumni's contributions.
    Plural nouns ending in s: Add only an apostrophe—the companies' concerns.
    Singular nouns not ending in s: Add 's—the committee's members.
    Singular common nouns ending in s: Add 's unless the next word begins with s—the witness's testimony; the witness' story.
    Singular proper names ending in s: Use only an apostrophe—Frank Lovass' company.

Colon

- Colons are most commonly used to introduce lists or items in a series. Capitalize the first word after a colon only if it marks the beginning of a complete sentence:

    The consultant recommended the following: Handle discharge planning prior to admission.
    He had only one fear: a malpractice suit.

(**Note:** You will have to fight programs like Word to accept a lower case letter after a colon.)

- In headlines and subheads, capitalize the first letter after a colon, even if it would not normally be capitalized:

    Observations: Positive Notes

- Items in a series following a colon that punctuates an incomplete sentence introducing the series should begin with lower case and end in a semicolon or comma. End the next to last item with "and"; end the last item with a period:

    To comply with the new HCFA requirement, administrators must:

    > *identify performing, referring and ordering physicians;*
    > *list departments, affiliated clinics and physician offices; and*
    > *specify which of each category comes under the ruling.*

(**Note:** For a series of bullet items, punctuation following each item is not necessary unless the items are, themselves, complete sentences requiring a period.)

Comma

- Use commas to separate items in a series, but not before the conjunction:

    Students major in several areas, including electrical, mechanical and chemical engineering.

(**Note:** Putting a comma before the conjunction [and, or] is optional in modern usage. But be *consistent* in your choice within a document.)

- Use a comma to separate the independent clauses of a compound sentence (two independent clauses joined by a conjunction):

    The first experiment was successful, and a second was begun.

- Do not use a comma to separate two verb phrases when the subject is the same for both:

    We can produce innovative technology and protect patients at the same time.

- Use commas to set off a nonrestrictive appositive phrase:

    Carl Evans, a USF researcher, announced his discovery of a new energy source.

- Use a comma after an introductory phrase, unless it is very short:

    During the first day of operation, the staff functioned efficiently.

- Use commas to set off complete dates:

    The clinic is scheduled for an April 3, 2003, opening.

- Use commas to separate city and state in a sentence:

    In Coalville, Kentucky, the clinic offers free medical care.

- Do not use commas in dates where only the month and year are given:

    The clinic opened in April 1988.

- Do not use a comma to set off "Jr." in a name or "Inc." after a company name (unless the person or company specifically uses a comma):

    Carl Brenner Jr. is now chairman of TechMate Inc.

Dash

- Do not overuse dashes: they can clutter the flow of the text.

- A dash may be used to indicate a shift in thought or to isolate parenthetical material:

    The new course—the first in this area of study—finally won university approval.

Ellipsis

- Use an ellipsis (...) to indicate the omission of quoted material, with a space between an ellipsis and the word it follows or precedes:

    President Jones said his first year was "a total ... success" from his perspective.

- Use an ellipsis and a period when an ellipsis ends a sentence. In this example, the fourth "period," immediately after "patients," is the sentence period:

    The FDA said the product offered "enormous potential for the benefit of patients. ..."

Hyphen

- As a general rule, avoid compound modifiers when a single modifier will do. When they are necessary, most compound modifiers should be hyphenated:

    high-speed line; long-term plan; ill-fated project

- Hyphenate compound modifiers consisting of a number and unit of measurement:

    10-mile altitude; 18-month study

- Do not hyphenate compound modifiers whose words appear in a normal sequence or form a commonly used phrase:

    basic research budget; medical insurance company

(**Note:** Do not hyphenate adverb/adjective phrases—e.g., "commonly used.")

- Use suspensive hyphenation (i.e., when the first element of two is hyphenated as well) when needed:

    10- to 20-member committee

Parentheses/brackets

- Parentheses, like dashes, should be used judiciously. Before using parentheses, consider whether the idea would be better stated as a separate sentence. If it is written as a phrase, consider whether it would be best set off by commas.

- Use brackets " [ ] " within a quoted phrase to indicate that the bracketed words are not those of the person quoted:

    The chairman said he was "very pleased with [the committee's] progress" in considering the new rule proposal.

Punctuating Quotations

- Set off a direct quote with a comma:

    "Diabetes is a geneticist's nightmare," Belcher says.

- Do not use a comma to set off an indirect quotation introduced by "whether," "if," "that" or similar conjunctions:

    Belcher said that "diabetes is a geneticist's nightmare."

Quotation Marks

- Place periods and commas *inside* quotation marks:

    "All good things," he said, "must come to an end."

- Place colons, semicolons and question marks *outside* quotation marks, unless they are part of the quoted material:

    Who said, "Only the good die young"?

- Use quotation marks for titles of articles in periodicals, chapter titles and individual selections in books. Use italics—or underscoring—for references to the publications themselves:

    Chapter One, "The Curse of the Frantic Tax Man," is a worthy start for Benton's new book, <u>Cry and the World Cries with You</u>.

(**Note:** With computer programs, use italics as opposed to underscoring. After all, underscoring was used traditionally to tell typesetters to *use* italics.)

Semicolon

- Use a semicolon to separate statements of contrast and closely related statements when they are not joined by a conjunction. The statements should be able to stand alone as sentences:

    It was the best of times; it was the worst of times.
    The medical record greatly aids coding; it should be consulted often.

- Use a semicolon to separate items in a series that is long and complex or involves internal punctuation:

    The law firms involved in the suit are Long, Wendy and Boring; Catcham, Trium and Jailem; and Weasle, Ratt and Finque Ltd.

- Place a semicolon outside quotes:

    The reporter said the meeting was "long and boring"; however, she did offer a positive review of its content.

STYLE AND USAGE

Abbreviations

- Abbreviate "U.S." (with periods) when used as an adjective, but spell out when used as a noun:

    U.S. hospitals; doctors from the United States

- Abbreviate states when used with the name of a city or in reference to a Member of Congress. Do not abbreviate when used alone or for the inside address of a letter. Use the following state abbreviations:

Alabama	*AL*	*Montana*	*MT*
Alaska	*AK*	*Nebraska*	*NE*
Arizona	*AZ*	*Nevada*	*NV*
Arkansas	*AR*	*New Hampshire*	*NH*
California	*CA*	*New Jersey*	*NJ*
Colorado	*CO*	*New Mexico*	*NM*
Connecticut	*CT*	*New York*	*NY*
Delaware	*DE*	*North Carolina*	*NC*
District of Columbia	*DC*	*North Dakota*	*ND*
Florida	*FL*	*Ohio*	*OH*
Georgia	*GA*	*Oklahoma*	*OK*
Guam	*GM*	*Oregon*	*OR*
Hawaii	*HI*	*Pennsylvania*	*PA*
Idaho	*ID*	*Puerto Rico*	*PR*
Illinois	*IL*	*Rhode Island*	*RI*
Indiana	*IN*	*South Carolina*	*SC*
Iowa	*IA*	*South Dakota*	*SD*
Kansas	*KS*	*Tennessee*	*TN*
Kentucky	*KY*	*Texas*	*TX*
Louisiana	*LA*	*Utah*	*UT*
Maine	*ME*	*Vermont*	*VT*
Maryland	*MD*	*Virginia*	*VA*
Massachusetts	*MA*	*Virgin Islands*	*VI*
Michigan	*MI*	*Washington*	*WA*
Minnesota	*MN*	*West Virginia*	*WV*
Mississippi	*MS*	*Wisconsin*	*WI*
Missouri	*MO*	*Wyoming*	*WY*

- Months:

Jan.	July
Feb.	Aug.
March	Sept.
April	Oct.
May	Nov.
June	Dec.

(**Note:** In formal business correspondence, it is best to spell out the month: September 1989; September 21, 1993.)

Acronyms

- Use capital letters for acronyms. Spell out the entity or term in the first reference, with the acronym following in parentheses:

    the University of South Florida (USF)

- Do not use periods between the letters in an acronym.

- As a general rule, if a term or entity occurs only once, don't use the acronym. An exception would be in reference to an entity you know to be familiar to your readers (e.g., NASA).

- When an acronym is used as a noun, it does not require an article before it:

    USF announced a new enrollment plan today.

Collective Nouns

- Nouns that denote a *unit* take singular verbs and pronouns (e.g., class, committee, group):

    The committee is meeting to set its agenda.

- Some words that are plural in form become collective nouns and take singular verbs when the group or quantity is regarded as a unit:

    The data is sound. (A unit)
    The data have been carefully collected. (Individual items)
    The marketing staff is on the job. (A unit)
    Staff are doing their best to meet the deadline. (Individuals)

Correlative Expressions (both, and; not only, but also; either, or; first, second, third)

- Correlative expressions should be followed by the same grammatical construction:

    You can either accept our offer or reject it.
    His assertion is both baseless and pointless.

E.g./i.e.

- "E.g." means "for example"; "i.e." means "that is." Both are followed by a comma:

    There are several new rules, e.g., those governing classroom use, that apply here.
    The additional cost of doing business, i.e., through higher taxes, is controversial.

Fewer/less

- "Fewer" refers to numbers:

    That building has fewer floors.

- "Less" refers to amount or weight:

    There is less water in this glass.

It's/its

- "It's" is a contraction for "it is":

    It's too late to change the text now.

- "Its" is the possessive case of "it":

    Its main attraction is the new plumbing.

Numbers

- Write numbers from zero to ten as words and numbers above ten as figures.

- When several numbers appear in the same sentence or paragraph, express them alike, regardless of other rules and guidelines:

    The company owned 150 trucks, employed 267 people and rented 7 warehouses.

- Spell out numbers that begin a sentence, even if they would otherwise be written as figures:

    One hundred fifty-three people attended the meeting.

(**Note:** If spelling the number out seems awkward, try rewriting the sentence: *A crowd of 153 people attended the meeting.*)

Pronoun Agreement

- Pronouns should agree in number (singular or plural) with their antecedents:

    Anyone who fails to carry automobile insurance should have his or her head examined.

- To avoid using "his or her" too often, which can become awkward, alternate the gender reference in your document, if appropriate:

    The patient should leave his identification with the admissions clerk.
    A patient should not leave her valuables unattended.

- Much of the confusion regarding pronoun agreement can be avoided by using the plural form of the noun (e.g., "patients" instead of "a patient") when possible. The important point to remember is *not* to mix singular and plural:

    <u>Not</u>: Each patient should get their own charts.
    <u>But</u>: Patients should get their own charts.

Pronoun Case

- "I" is the subjective case; "me" is the objective case. Use "I" as the subject of a sentence and "me" as the direct or indirect object of the sentence or the object of a preposition:

    Between you and me, I think he should leave.

(**Note:** If you're confused, substitute the plural form as a quick check. You wouldn't say "Between we," would you?)

- "Myself" is the reflexive form of the pronoun (i.e., it "reflects" the pronoun preceding it):

    I gave myself the job.

(**Note:** Do not use the reflexive [-self] form in place of either the subjective or objective form:

    <u>Not</u>: She assigned the job to Frank, Lorraine and myself.
    <u>But</u>: She assigned the job to Frank, Lorraine and me.

Split Infinitive

- Avoid splitting the infinitive form of a verb (as much as possible anyway):

    <u>Not</u>: To boldly go where no man has gone before. (I know, but Kirk was not infallible, was he?)
    <u>But</u>: To go boldly where no one has gone before. (This is what we would have heard if Spock were doing the voice-over!)

That, Which

- "Which" normally refers to things, "who" to persons and "that" to either persons or things.

- "That" introduces a restrictive or defining clause that cannot be omitted from the sentence without losing the meaning:

    The river that flows between D.C. and Virginia is the Potomac.

- "Which" introduces a nonessential or parenthetical clause, set off by commas, which could be omitted:

    The Potomac River, which flows between D.C. and Virginia, is muddy.

- When in doubt, it helps to read the sentence aloud. If you pause naturally before the relative pronoun, it probably should be "which," and the clause should be set off by commas.

Their/there/they're

- "Their" is the plural possessive of "they":

    The companies got their questions answered.

- "There" is an indication of place, among other meanings:

    Put the manual there, please.

- "They're" is a contraction of "they are":

    They're going to return shortly.

Your/you're

- "Your" is the possessive form of "you":

    You will need your briefcase.

- "You're" is a contraction of "you are":

    You're going to be late.

Who/whom; Who's/whose

- "Who" is the subjective case; "whom" is the objective case:

    Who is the chairman of this committee?
    To whom should I give this memo?

- "Who's" is the contraction of "who is"; "whose" is the possessive form:

    Who's responsible for this mess?
    Whose notepad is this?

Writing Style

Active vs. Passive Voice

Keep sentences in active voice whenever possible:

> *Not*: The report <u>was issued by</u> the Health Care Financing Administration.
> *But*: The Health Care Financing Administration <u>issued</u> the report.

Audience

Always be aware of the audience for whom you are writing. Among other considerations, you should have a good idea of your audience's level of familiarity with the subject matter, which will dictate how much explanation you need to provide.

Brevity

Explain thoroughly, but avoid using 10 words when 5 will do:

> *Not*: When coders took the time to examine medical records in depth, coding was optimized and reimbursement increased twofold.
> *But*: Coders doubled reimbursement by checking medical records thoroughly.

(**Note:** Using the active voice and avoiding unnecessary adjectives and adverbs can streamline writing.)

Tone

Writing is like clothing: It should be appropriate for the occasion. You wouldn't wear a tuxedo or a formal evening gown to a picnic, or cut-offs to a presidential reception. Unnecessarily formal writing can appear stilted to a reader expecting an informal response to a simple question, and writing that is too informal might offend a reader expecting a formal response outlining your company's plans for development.

English as a Second Language

Non-native English speakers often have problems with various patterns of usage in the language. While problems can occur in many areas, the following are the more common ones I have noted in students for whom English is a second (or third or fourth) language. The list is by no means exhaustive.

Articles (a/an, the)

In many languages nouns have articles attached to them already, indicating gender and number (e.g., das Boot or les miserables). English nouns exist on their own; therefore, it is necessary to attach an article in many cases:

Bring me the books on the shelf.

To confuse the issue, there are times when nouns do *not* require an article:

Books are essential for any student.

This means you must consider the placement of the noun in the sentence as well as its use:

The book I admire most is Of Mice and Men.

Remember, too, that "a" and "an" are general articles (e.g., Bring me *a* book), while "the" is a specific article (e.g., That is *the* book I want).

Idioms

Idioms are phrases or constructions that have a meaning different from the literal. They are understood by native speakers of a language, but can be confusing to others. For example, the expression "out of sight, out of mind" was once translated by a non-native English speaker to mean "blind idiot." Literally, that translation makes sense: "Out of sight" (e.g., sightless) could mean blind, and "out of mind" (e.g., without thought capacity) could mean "idiot." The key is to know the cultural understanding of an idiom before using it. When in doubt, avoid using idioms.

Plural spellings

In English, the plural of most nouns is formed by adding an "s" or "es" to the singular spelling of a noun:

Singular: "floor"
Plural: "floors"

There are exceptions, of course (e.g., the plural of "man" is "men"). Most non-native English speakers seem to have more trouble with dropping the plural "s" than with spelling the plurals of words that change form, such as man/men.

Prepositions

Non-native English speakers sometimes confuse English prepositions. Be sure you understand the meaning of the prepositions you use. There is a big difference, for example, between being "*on* the floor" and being "*in* the floor."

Appendix 1

Engineering Codes of Ethics

INSTITUTE OF ELECTRICAL AND ELECTRONICS ENGINEERS (IEEE) CODE OF ETHICS

We, the members of the IEEE, in recognition of the importance of our technologies in affecting the quality of life throughout the world, and in accepting a personal obligation to our profession, its members and the communities we serve, do hereby commit ourselves to the highest ethical and professional conduct and agree:

1. to accept responsibility in making engineering decisions consistent with the safety, health and welfare of the public, and to disclose promptly factors that might endanger the public or the environment;
2. to avoid real or perceived conflicts of interest whenever possible, and to disclose them to affected parties when they do exist;
3. to be honest and realistic in stating claims or estimates based on available data;
4. to reject bribery in all its forms;
5. to improve the understanding of technology, its appropriate application, and potential consequences;
6. to maintain and improve our technical competence and to undertake technological tasks for others only if qualified by training or experience, or after full disclosure of pertinent limitations;
7. to seek, accept, and offer honest criticism of technical work, to acknowledge and correct errors, and to credit properly the contributions of others;
8. to treat fairly all persons regardless of such factors as race, religion, gender, disability, age, or national origin;
9. to avoid injuring others, their property, reputation, or employment by false or malicious action;
10. to assist colleagues and co-workers in their professional development and to support them in following this code of ethics.

—Approved by the IEEE Board of Directors, August 1990

© 2001 IEEE. Reprinted with permission of the IEEE.

American Society of Mechanical Engineers (ASME) Code of Ethics of Engineers

The Fundamental Principles

Engineers uphold and advance the integrity, honor, and dignity of the Engineering profession by:

I. using their knowledge and skill for the enhancement of human welfare;
II. being honest and impartial, and serving with fidelity the public, their employers and clients; and
III. striving to increase the competence and prestige of the engineering profession.

The Fundamental Canons

1. Engineers shall hold paramount the safety, health and welfare of the public in the performance of their professional duties.
2. Engineers shall perform services only in areas of their competence.
3. Engineers shall continue their professional development throughout their careers and shall provide opportunities for the professional development of those engineers under their supervision.
4. Engineers shall act in professional matters for each employer or client as faithful agents or trustees, and shall avoid conflicts of interest.
5. Engineers shall build their professional reputation on the merit of their services and shall not compete unfairly with others.
6. Engineers shall associate only with reputable persons or organizations.
7. Engineers shall issue public statements only in an objective and truthful manner.

National Society of Professional Engineers (NSPE) Code of Ethics for Engineers

Preamble

Engineering is an important and learned profession. As members of this profession, engineers are expected to exhibit the highest standards of honesty and integrity. Engineering has a direct and vital impact on the quality of life for all people. Accordingly, the services provided by engineers require honesty, impartiality, fairness and equity, and must be dedicated to the protection of the public health, safety, and welfare. Engineers must perform under a standard of professional behavior that requires adherence to the highest principles of ethical conduct.

Code of Ethics of the America Society of Mechanical Engineers. Reprinted by permission of the American Society of Mechanical Engineers.
Code of Ethics of the National Society of Professional Engineers. Reprinted by permission.

I. Fundamental Canons
Engineers, in the fulfillment of their professional duties, shall:

1. Hold paramount the safety, health and welfare of the public.
2. Perform services only in areas of their competence.
3. Issue public statements only in an objective and truthful manner.
4. Act for each employer or client as faithful agents or trustees.
5. Avoid deceptive acts.
6. Conduct themselves honorably, responsibly, ethically, and lawfully so as to enhance the honor, reputation, and usefulness of the profession.

II. Rules of Practice

1. Engineers shall hold paramount the safety, health, and welfare of the public.
   a. If engineers' judgment is overruled under circumstances that endanger life or property, they shall notify their employer or client and such other authority as may be appropriate.
   b. Engineers shall approve only those engineering documents that are in conformity with applicable standards.
   c. Engineers shall not reveal facts, data or information without the prior consent of the client or employer except as authorized or required by law or this Code.
   d. Engineers shall not permit the use of their name or associate in business ventures with any person or firm that they believe are engaged in fraudulent or dishonest enterprise.
   e. Engineers having knowledge of any alleged violation of this Code shall report thereon to appropriate professional bodies and, when relevant, also to public authorities, and cooperate with the proper authorities in furnishing such information or assistance as may be required.

2. Engineers shall perform services only in the areas of their competence.
   a. Engineers shall undertake assignments only when qualified by education or experience in the specific technical fields involved.
   b. Engineers shall not affix their signatures to any plans or documents dealing with subject matter in which they lack competence, nor to any plan or document not prepared under their direction and control.
   c. Engineers may accept assignments and assume responsibility for coordination of an entire project and sign and seal the engineering documents for the entire project, provided that each technical segment is signed and sealed only by the qualified engineers who prepared the segment.

3. Engineers shall issue public statements only in an objective and truthful manner.
   a. Engineers shall be objective and truthful in professional reports, statements, or testimony. They shall include all relevant and pertinent information in such reports, statements, or testimony, which should bear the date indicating when it was current.
   b. Engineers may express publicly technical opinions that are founded upon knowledge of the facts and competence in the subject matter.
   c. Engineers shall issue no statements, criticisms, or arguments on technical matters that are inspired or paid for by interested parties, unless they have prefaced their comments by explicitly identifying the interested parties on whose behalf they are speaking, and by revealing the existence of any interest the engineers may have in the matters.

4. Engineers shall act for each employer or client as faithful agents or trustees.
    a. Engineers shall disclose all known or potential conflicts of interest that could influence or appear to influence their judgment or the quality of their services.
    b. Engineers shall not accept compensation, financial or otherwise, from more than one party for services on the same project, or for services pertaining to the same project, unless the circumstances are fully disclosed and agreed to by all interested parties.
    c. Engineers shall not solicit or accept financial or other valuable consideration, directly or indirectly, from outside agents in connection with the work for which they are responsible.
    d. Engineers in public service as members, advisors, or employees of a governmental or quasi-governmental body or department shall not participate in decisions with respect to services solicited or provided by them or their organizations in private or public engineering practice.
    e. Engineers shall not solicit or accept a contract from a governmental body on which a principal or officer of their organization serves as a member.

5. Engineers shall avoid deceptive acts.
    a. Engineers shall not falsify their qualifications or permit misrepresentation of their or their associates' qualifications. They shall not misrepresent or exaggerate their responsibility in or for the subject matter of prior assignments. Brochures or other presentations incident to the solicitation of employment shall not misrepresent pertinent facts concerning employers, employees, associates, joint venturers, or past accomplishments.
    b. Engineers shall not offer, give, solicit or receive, either directly or indirectly, any contribution to influence the award of a contract by public authority, or which may be reasonably construed by the public as having the effect of intent to influencing the awarding of a contract. They shall not offer any gift or other valuable consideration in order to secure work. They shall not pay a commission, percentage, or brokerage fee in order to secure work, except to a bona fide employee or bona fide established commercial or marketing agencies retained by them.

III. Professional Obligations

1. Engineers shall be guided in all their relations by the highest standards of honesty and integrity.
    a. Engineers shall acknowledge their errors and shall not distort or alter the facts.
    b. Engineers shall advise their clients or employers when they believe a project will not be successful.
    c. Engineers shall not accept outside employment to the detriment of their regular work or interest. Before accepting any outside engineering employment they will notify their employers.
    d. Engineers shall not attempt to attract an engineer from another employer by false or misleading pretenses.
    e. Engineers shall not promote their own interest at the expense of the dignity and integrity of the profession.

2. Engineers shall at all times strive to serve the public interest.
    a. Engineers shall seek opportunities to participate in civic affairs; career guidance for youths; and work for the advancement of the safety, health and well-being of their community.
    b. Engineers shall not complete, sign, or seal plans and/or specifications that are not in conformity with applicable engineering standards. If the client or employer insists on such unprofessional conduct, they shall notify the proper authorities and withdraw from further service on the project.
    c. Engineers shall endeavor to extend public knowledge and appreciation of engineering and its achievements.

3. Engineers shall avoid all conduct or practice that deceives the public.
   a. Engineers shall avoid the use of statements containing a material misrepresentation of fact or omitting a material fact.
   b. Consistent with the foregoing, Engineers may advertise for recruitment of personnel.
   c. Consistent with the foregoing, Engineers may prepare articles for the lay or technical press, but such articles shall not imply credit to the author for work performed by others.

4. Engineers shall not disclose, without consent, confidential information concerning the business affairs or technical processes of any present or former client or employer, or public body on which they serve.
   a. Engineers shall not, without the consent of all interested parties, promote or arrange for new employment or practice in connection with a specific project for which the Engineer has gained particular and specialized knowledge.
   b. Engineers shall not, without the consent of all interested parties, participate in or represent an adversary interest in connection with a specific project or proceeding in which the Engineer has gained particular specialized knowledge on behalf of a former client or employer.

5. Engineers shall not be influenced in their professional duties by conflicting interests.
   a. Engineers shall not accept financial or other considerations, including free engineering designs, from material or equipment suppliers for specifying their product.
   b. Engineers shall not accept commissions or allowances, directly or indirectly, from contractors or other parties dealing with clients or employers of the Engineer in connection with work for which the Engineer is responsible.

6. Engineers shall not attempt to obtain employment or advancement or professional engagements by untruthfully criticizing other engineers, or by other improper or questionable methods.
   a. Engineers shall not request, propose, or accept a commission on a contingent basis under circumstances in which their judgment may be compromised.
   b. Engineers in salaried positions shall accept part-time engineering work only to the extent consistent with policies of the employer and in accordance with ethical considerations.
   c. Engineers shall not, without consent, use equipment, supplies, laboratory, or office facilities of an employer to carry on outside private practice.

7. Engineers shall not attempt to injure, maliciously or falsely, directly or indirectly, the professional reputation, prospects, practice, or employment of other engineers. Engineers who believe others are guilty of unethical or illegal practice shall present such information to the proper authority for action.
   a. Engineers in private practice shall not review the work of another engineer for the same client, except with the knowledge of such engineer, or unless the connection of such engineer with the work has been terminated.
   b. Engineers in governmental, industrial, or educational employ are entitled to review and evaluate the work of other engineers when so required by their employment duties.
   c. Engineers in sales or industrial employ are entitled to make engineering comparisons of represented products with products of other suppliers.

8. Engineers shall accept personal responsibility for their professional activities, provided, however, that Engineers may seek indemnification for services arising out of their practice for other than gross negligence, where the Engineer's interests cannot otherwise be protected.
   a. Engineers shall conform with state registration laws in the practice of engineering.
   b. Engineers shall not use association with a nonengineer, a corporation, or partnership as a "cloak" for unethical acts.

9. Engineers shall give credit for engineering work to those to whom credit is due, and will recognize the proprietary interests of others.
    a. Engineers shall, whenever possible, name the person or persons who may be individually responsible for designs, inventions, writings, or other accomplishments.
    b. Engineers using designs supplied by a client recognize that the designs remain the property of the client and may not be duplicated by the Engineer for others without express permission.
    c. Engineers, before undertaking work for others in connection with which the Engineer may make improvements, plans, designs, inventions, or other records that may justify copyrights or patents, should enter into a positive agreement regarding ownership.
    d. Engineers' designs, data, records, and notes referring exclusively to an employer's work are the employer's property. Employer should indemnify the Engineer for use of the information for any purpose other than the original purpose.

As Revised February 2001

AMERICAN INSTITUTE OF CHEMICAL ENGINEERS CODE OF ETHICS

The Board of Directors of the American Institute of Chemical Engineers adopted this Code of Ethics to which it expects that the professional conduct of its members shall conform, and to which every applicant attests by signing his or her membership application.

Members of the American Institute of Chemical Engineers shall uphold and advance the integrity, honor, and dignity of the engineering profession by: being honest and impartial and serving with fidelity their employers, their clients, and the public; striving to increase the competence and prestige of the engineering profession; and using their knowledge and skill for the enhancement of human welfare. To achieve these goals, members shall:

- Hold paramount the safety, health, and welfare of the public in performance of their professional duties.
- Formally advise their employers or clients (and consider further disclosure, if warranted) if they perceive that a consequence of their duties will adversely affect the present or future health or safety of their colleagues or the public.
- Accept responsibility for their actions and recognize the contributions of others; seek critical review of their work and offer objective criticism of the work of others.
- Issue statements or present information only in an objective and truthful manner.
- Act in professional matters for each employer or client as faithful agents or trustees, and avoid conflicts of interest.
- Treat fairly all colleagues and co-workers, recognizing their unique contributions and capabilities.
- Perform professional services only in areas of their competence.
- Build their professional reputations on the merits of their services.
- Continue their professional development throughout their careers, and provide opportunities for the professional development of those under their supervision.

Code of Ethics of the American Institute of Chemical Engineers. Reprinted by permission.

Association of Computing Machinery (ACM) Code of Ethics

1. General Moral Imperatives.

As an ACM member I will ...

1.1 Contribute to society and human well-being.

This principle concerning the quality of life of all people affirms an obligation to protect fundamental human rights and to respect the diversity of all cultures. An essential aim of computing professionals is to minimize negative consequences of computing systems, including threats to health and safety. When designing or implementing systems, computing professionals must attempt to ensure that the products of their efforts will be used in socially responsible ways, will meet social needs, and will avoid harmful effects to health and welfare.

In addition to a safe social environment, human well-being includes a safe natural environment. Therefore, computing professionals who design and develop systems must be alert to, and make others aware of, any potential damage to the local or global environment.

1.2 Avoid harm to others.

"Harm" means injury or negative consequences, such as undesirable loss of information, loss of property, property damage, or unwanted environmental impacts. This principle prohibits use of computing technology in ways that result in harm to any of the following: users, the general public, employees, employers. Harmful actions include intentional destruction or modification of files and programs leading to serious loss of resources or unnecessary expenditure of human resources such as the time and effort required to purge systems of computer viruses.

Well-intended actions, including those that accomplish assigned duties, may lead to harm unexpectedly. In such an event, the responsible person or persons are obligated to undo or mitigate the negative consequences as much as possible. One way to avoid unintentional harm is to carefully consider potential impacts on all those affected by decisions made during design and implementation.

To minimize the possibility of indirectly harming others, computing professionals must minimize malfunctions by following generally accepted standards for system design and testing. Furthermore, it is often necessary to assess the social consequences of systems to project the likelihood of any serious harm to others. If system features are misrepresented to users, coworkers, or supervisors, the individual computing professional is responsible for any resulting injury.

In the work environment, the computing professional has the additional obligation to report any signs of system dangers that might result in serious personal or social damage. If one's superiors do not act to curtail or mitigate such dangers, it may be necessary to "blow the whistle" to help correct the problem or reduce the risk. However, capricious or misguided reporting of violations can, itself, be harmful. Before reporting violations, all relevant aspects of the incident must be thoroughly assessed. In particular, the assessment of risk and responsibility must be credible. It is suggested that advice be sought from other computing professionals. (See principle 2.5 regarding thorough evaluations.)

1.3 Be honest and trustworthy.

Honesty is an essential component of trust. Without trust an organization cannot function effectively. The honest computing professional will not make deliberately false or deceptive claims about a system or system design but will instead provide full disclosure of all pertinent system limitations and problems.

Reprinted from *Communications of the ACM*, Vol. 36:2, February 1993, courtesy of the Association for Computing Machinery.

A computer professional has a duty to be honest about his or her own qualifications and about any circumstances that might lead to conflicts of interest.

Membership in volunteer organizations such as ACM may at times place individuals in situations where their statements or actions could be interpreted as carrying the "weight" of a larger group of professionals. An ACM member will exercise care to not misrepresent ACM or positions and policies of ACM or any ACM units.

1.4 Be fair and take action not to discriminate.

The values of equality, tolerance, respect for others, and the principles of equal justice govern this imperative. Discrimination on the basis of race, sex, religion, age, disability, national origin, or other such factors is an explicit violation of ACM policy and will not be tolerated.

Inequities between different groups of people may result from the misuse of information and technology. In a fair society all individuals would have equal opportunity to participate in, or benefit from, the use of computer resources regardless of race, sex, religion, age, disability, national origin or other such similar factors. However, these ideals do not justify unauthorized use of computer resources nor do they provide an adequate basis for violation of any other ethical imperatives of this code.

1.5 Honor property rights including copyrights and patents.

Violation of copyrights, patents, trade secrets and the terms of license agreements is prohibited by law in most circumstances. Even when software is not so protected, such violations are contrary to professional behavior. Copies of software should be made only with proper authorization. Unauthorized duplication of materials must not be condoned.

1.6 Give proper credit for intellectual property.

Computing professionals are obligated to protect the integrity of intellectual property. Specifically, one must not take credit for other's ideas or work, even in cases where the work has not been explicitly protected, for example by copyright or patent.

1.7 Respect the privacy of others.

Computing and communication technology enables the collection and exchange of personal information on a scale unprecedented in the history of civilization. Thus there is increased potential for violating the privacy of individuals and groups. It is the responsibility of professionals to maintain the privacy and integrity of data describing individuals. This includes taking precautions to ensure the accuracy of data, as well as protecting it from unauthorized access or accidental disclosure to inappropriate individuals. Furthermore, procedures must be established to allow individuals to review their records and correct inaccuracies.

This imperative implies that only the necessary amount of personal information be collected in a system, that retention and disposal periods for that information be clearly defined and enforced, and that personal information gathered for a specific purpose not be used for other purposes without consent of the individual(s). These principles apply to electronic communications, including electronic mail, and prohibit procedures that capture or monitor electronic user data, including messages, without the permission of users or bona fide authorization related to system operation and maintenance. User data observed during the normal duties of system operation and maintenance must be treated with strictest confidentiality except in cases where it is evidence for the violation of law, organizational regulations, or this code. In these cases, the nature or contents of that information must be disclosed only to proper authorities.

1.8 Honor confidentiality.

The principle of honesty extends to issues of confidentiality of information whenever one has made an explicit promise to honor confidentiality or, implicitly, when private information not directly related to the performance of one's duties becomes available. The ethical concern is to respect all obligations of confidentiality to employers, clients, and users unless discharged from such obligations by requirements of the law or other principles of this Code.

2. More Specific Professional Responsibilities.

As an ACM computing professional I will ...

2.1 Strive to achieve the highest quality, effectiveness and dignity in both the process and products of professional work.

Excellence is perhaps the most important obligation of a professional. The computing professional must strive to achieve quality and to be cognizant of the serious negative consequences that may result from poor quality in a system.

2.2 Acquire and maintain professional competence.

Excellence depends on individuals who take responsibility for acquiring and maintaining professional competence. A professional must participate in setting standards for appropriate levels of competence and strive to achieve those standards. Upgrading technical knowledge and competence can be achieved in several ways: doing independent study; attending seminars, conferences, or courses; and being involved in professional organizations.

2.3 Know and respect existing laws pertaining to professional work.

ACM members must obey existing local, state, province, national, and international laws unless there is a compelling ethical basis not to do so. Policies and procedures of the organization in which one participates must also be obeyed. But compliance must be balanced with the recognition that sometimes existing laws and rules may be immoral or inappropriate and, therefore, must be challenged.

Violation of a law or regulation may be ethical when that law or rule has inadequate moral basis or when it conflicts with another law judged to be more important. If one decides to violate law or rule because it is viewed as unethical, or for any other reason, one must fully accept responsibility for one's actions and for the consequences.

2.4 Accept and provide appropriate professional review.

Quality professional work, especially in the computing profession, depends on professional reviewing and critiquing. Whenever appropriate, individual members should seek and utilize peer review as well as provide critical review of the work of others.

2.5 Give comprehensive and thorough evaluations of computer systems and their impacts, including analysis of possible risks.

Computer professionals must strive to be perceptive, thorough, and objective when evaluating, recommending, and presenting system descriptions and alternatives. Computer professionals are in a position of special trust and therefore have a special responsibility to provide objective, credible evaluations to employers, clients, users, and the public. When providing evaluations, the professional must also identify any relevant conflicts of interest, as stated in imperative 1.3.

As noted in the discussion of principle 1.2 on avoiding harm, any signs of danger from systems must be reported to those who have opportunity and/or responsibility to resolve them. See the guidelines for imperative 1.2 for more details concerning harm, including the reporting of professional violations.

2.6 Honor contracts, agreements, and assigned responsibilities.

Honoring one's commitments is a matter of integrity and honesty. For the computer professional this includes ensuring that system elements perform as intended. Also, when one contracts for work with another party, one has an obligation to keep that party properly informed about progress toward completing that work.

A computing professional has a responsibility to request a change in any assignment that he or she feels cannot be completed as defined. Only after serious consideration and with full disclosure of risks and concerns to the employer or client, should one accept the assignment. The major underlying principle here is the obligation to accept personal accountability for professional work. On some occasions other ethical principles may take the greater priority.

A judgment that a specific assignment should not be performed may not be accepted. Having clearly identified one's concerns and reasons for that judgment but failing to procure a change in that assignment, one may yet be obligated, by contract or by law, to proceed as directed. The computing professional's ethical judgment should be the final guide in deciding whether or not to proceed. Regardless of the decision, one must accept the responsibility for the consequences. However, performing assignments "against one's own judgment" does not relieve the professional of responsibility for any negative consequences.

2.7 Improve public understanding of computing and its consequences.

Computing professionals have a responsibility to share technical knowledge with the public by encouraging understanding of computing, including the impacts of computer systems and their limitations. This imperative implies an obligation to counter any false views related to computing.

2.8 Access computing and communication resources only when authorized to do so.

Theft or destruction of tangible and electronic property is prohibited by imperative 1.2—"Avoid harm to others." Trespassing and unauthorized use of a computer or communication system is addressed by this imperative. Trespassing includes accessing communication networks and computer systems, or accounts and/or files associated with those systems, without explicit authorization to do so. Individuals and organizations have the right to restrict access to their systems so long as they do not violate the discrimination principle (see 1.4).

No one should enter or use another's computing system, software, or data files without permission. One must always have appropriate approval before using system resources, including communication ports, file space, other system peripherals, and computer time.

3. Organizational Leadership Imperatives.

As an ACM member and an organizational leader, I will ...

3.1 Articulate social responsibilities of members of an organizational unit and encourage full acceptance of those responsibilities.

Because organizations of all kinds have impacts on the public, they must accept responsibilities to society. Organizational procedures and attitudes oriented toward quality and the welfare of society will reduce harm to members of the public, thereby serving public interest and fulfilling social responsibility. Therefore, organizational leaders must encourage full participation in meeting social responsibilities as well as quality performance.

3.2 Manage personnel and resources to design and build information systems that enhance the quality of working life.

Organizational leaders are responsible for ensuring that computer systems enhance, not degrade, the quality of working life. When implementing a computer system organizations must consider the personal and professional development, physical safety, and human dignity of all workers. Appropriate human-computer ergonomic standards should be considered in system design and in the workplace.

3.3 Acknowledge and support proper and authorized uses of an organization's computing and communications resources.

Because computer systems can become tools to harm as well as to benefit an organization, the leadership has the responsibility to clearly define appropriate and inappropriate uses of organizational computing resources. While the number and scope of such rules should be minimal, they should be fully enforced when established.

3.4 Ensure that users and those who will be affected by a system have their needs clearly articulated during the assessment and design of requirements; later the system must be validated to meet requirements.

Current system users, potential users and other persons whose lives may be affected by a system must have their needs assessed and incorporated in the statement of requirements. System validation should ensure compliance with those requirements.

3.5 Articulate and support policies that protect the dignity of users and others affected by a computing system.

Designing or implementing systems that deliberately or inadvertently demean individuals or groups is ethically unacceptable. Computer professionals who are in decision-making positions should verify that systems are designed and implemented to protect personal privacy and enhance personal dignity.

3.6 Create opportunities for members of the organization to learn the principles and limitations of computer systems.

This complements the imperative on public understanding (2.7). Educational opportunities are essential to facilitate optimal participation of all organizational members. Opportunities must be available to all members to help them improve their knowledge and skills in computing, including courses that familiarize them with the consequences and limitations of particular types of systems. In particular, professionals must be made aware of the dangers of building systems around oversimplified models, the improbability of anticipating and designing for every possible operating condition, and other issues related to the complexity of this profession.

4. Compliance with the Code.

As an ACM member I will ...

4.1 Uphold and promote the principles of this code.

The future of the computing profession depends on both technical and ethical excellence. Not only is it important for ACM computing professionals to adhere to the principles expressed in this Code, each member should encourage and support adherence by other members.

4.2 Treat violations of this code as inconsistent with membership in the ACM.

Adherence of professionals to a code of ethics is largely a voluntary matter. However, if a member does not follow this code by engaging in gross misconduct, membership in ACM may be terminated.

Appendix 2

Ethical Scenarios

Each of the scenarios below contains elements of an ethical conflict. Identify that conflict and suggest a response that is ethically sound. Be sure to include your analysis of what the ethical issue(s) is (are) and who the stakeholders are.

1. A competitor has just accused your company of plagiarizing your newest software program. It promises to be the best-selling product your company has developed. The head of your company's development team tells you that she did use some existing codes from the competitor's product in creating the program, but that those codes were supposed to be in the public domain. Your company rigorously supports the Software Engineers Code of Ethics. How would you respond to the accusations?

2. A part manufactured by your firm for NASA may have led to a failure during a critical stage of a shuttle launch. No one was killed, but there was considerable damage to the rocket/launch system. In researching the development and manufacture of the part, you discover some inter-office memos that suggest there might be a problem. Obviously senior management ignored those warnings. Another launch is being prepared using the same parts. What would you do? Who, if anyone, would you tell?

3. Your boss calls and asks you to prepare a brief explanation to the Board of Directors about why your company lost the bid for a major government project. You know the boss altered your recommendations for the bid. What would you tell the Board—and why? Where do your loyalties lie?

4. An employee working under you has told you he is worried about the stability of a critical waste control valve at your plant, and that no one he worked with seemed to be concerned. When you mention it to your manager, he says not to worry about it; everything is under control. A wildlife refuge, a school and several residences could be threatened if an accident occurs. What should you do?

5. A sub-contractor on a bridge project you are over-seeing suggests that using slightly less expensive materials in construction might save his company—and yours—a considerable amount of money. The materials he suggests substituting for the ones in the original bid are still within code. If the parts to be used are still up to standards, is there any harm in making the switch? If you do make the change, should you tell anyone? Who? Why?

6. You are the electrical engineer on a high-rise project. A pipe has burst on the tenth floor, causing major flooding on the ninth through sixth floors. There is concern that the electrical system for the building might be compromised. Preliminary testing shows that the system is still operational and within safety parameters, but you know problems could take days or weeks to develop. Reinstalling the system will put the project far behind schedule. What would you do?

SYSTEM REQUIREMENTS FOR THE CD

- Microsoft® Windows 95 or higher or
- Macintosh® OS 7.5.2 or higher;
- 64MB RAM

If your computer contains a version of Microsoft® PowerPoint® earlier than 2000, you may need to install the Microsoft® PowerPoint® Viewer included on the CD to properly view the presentations.